# More or Less
# Más o Menos
## Primary School Writings

*Volume I*

*Edited by*

**JOSEPH A. HAVILAND, MSEd**

outskirts
press

More or Less Más o Menos: Primary School Writings Volume 1
All Rights Reserved.
Copyright © 2016
Edited by Joseph A. Haviland, MSEd
v2.0 r1.1

Cover Photo © 2016 Joseph A. Haviland
All rights reserved - used with permission.

Outskirts Press, Inc.
http://www.outskirtspress.com

ISBN: 978-1-4787-7748-9

Outskirts Press and the "OP" logo are
trademarks belonging to Outskirts Press, Inc.

PRINTED IN THE UNITED STATES OF AMERICA

*"Live as if you were to die tomorrow.*
*Learn as if you were to live forever."*
— Mahatma Gandhi

Dedicated to Dr. Frederic Keith Gornell
(1945 – 2016)

Excerpted from Edition 10 of *Boston Way Newsletter*
March 2016

## OUR HEADMASTER

by

Ms. Isabel Sierra
&
Mr. Manuel Vinueza

"Great leaders communicate a vision that captures the imagination and fires the hearts and minds of those around them." Joseph B. Wirthlin

We say farewell to our beloved Headmaster, Dr. Frederic K. Gornell, a man with a warm smile and a profound conviction in students' holistic education.

As teachers, we are honored by the unique opportunity and great responsibility of being a positive change in our students' development. To achieve this goal, we follow his philosophy: not only do we nurture our students' scholarly minds but also their leadership skills that will lead them to success, their passion for research to understand their world, and their tolerance towards their peers.

Mr. Gornell made a difference in our lives; through his dedication and perseverance, he showed us that if we have a clear vision and a meaningful goal ahead, then in every day of our lives we will achieve happiness both at the personal and professional level. We can say with great conviction that by following his vision we – student, parents, faculty, and staff – win.

Let us never forget this man.

"One day I will find the right words, and they will be simple."
— Jack Kerouac

# Editor's Note

More or Less! (In Spanish it's *Más o Menos*.) It's an expression in Panama that I've heard a lot over the three years since my wife, Alicia, and I both came to live/teach here in February 2013. It assesses various things about the culture, from food to film to fashion to the latest fad.

More recently I heard it from one of my 4th grade students, Ricardo Alejandro, at Boston School International (BSI), who when I asked whether he was enjoying reading Michael Morpurgo's *An Elephant in the Garden*, from our class library, he responded, "More or less."

Now, I am a die hard Michael Morpurgo fan, and I know how expertly he crafts stories for both children and adults. So, my student saying "more or less" was his way of being nonchalantly affirmative about his assessment; high praise. It's part of being Panamanian, natural or adopted!

Truth be told, any really good book has moments of more or less. Long sentences mixed with short sentences to give contrast and flavorful flow to the writing. And as any successful publisher will tell you, every great story has conflict where characters are challenged or tested, mixed with times of peace and calm (tranquilo). More or less of each; flow and ebb!

With this collection of writing, we have bilingual older primary-age writers who have more to put down on paper with greater writing experience vs. very young bilingual writers, who are still testing their writing wings with less writing going on, but no less significant. Sometimes less becomes more in the way it resonates with the reader! This book is a mix of writing from haiku (Japanese poetry), to American cinquain, originally created by Adelaide Crapsey, an imagist poet, to realistic fiction, to life in space, to time travel to the future. It's all creatively childlike!

In each precious piece of writing found herewith, each student (some are trilingual) puts their best foot forward, regardless of age or grade level (1st - 5th) stringing words (palabras) together, while "speaking" his/her voice, more or less. That's what writing is; that's what this book is about. Enjoy! And congrats to students, parents, and staff at BSI who made this dream a reality.

Joseph A. Haviland, MSEd
Editor
Panama City, Panama
2016

# Introduction

Writing Movement at BSI
*Computers for Writing*
by
Ruth Mendoza

As a teacher, I believe that I'm part of a select group of people whose ultimate goal is to shape our society through our students. Throughout the years, I have witnessed how children become more technological and more critical about the world around them.

Through computer classes, this generation of children has acquired more logical and problem solving skills. Computer classes have opened up student creativity, their natural inquirer attributes, and their connectivity.

Our children know more about the world and are more open to expressing themselves. One way my primary students express themselves is through writing. I can see it in all ages.

Just in primary alone, from my 1st grade students who are just learning to write, all the way up to my 5th grade students, who are creating whole fantasy worlds with words, they are writing honestly about something each of them know or want to know (about the future).

What's wonderful to me is that my students are all using computers as the tool of choice to complete this process. As an example, in 1st grade, students are creating stories by using background images and inserting pictures about places they like to visit with their families. They have also created a booklet with riddles they have written. It's amazing how they start recognizing letters on the keyboard and discover that using high frequency words can create whole sentences.

The different computer projects, covered during the school year, equip students with computer/software tools to improve their overall writing process.

From PowerPoint presentations about countries to creating banners about cultural heritage or sending messages through emails to creating Edu blogs in Tbox Planet, the sky's the limit for students to demonstrate their ever-growing writing skills.

That's why I'm thrilled to see the creation of this book, *More or Less*. It's just one more way for our students to feel empowered with their writing.

## Principal's Page

I would like to personally thank all of the students and teachers for making *More or Less* the high-quality student publication which you are about to read. I would especially like to thank Teacher Joe Haviland for his tireless efforts in working with our teachers and students to make this publication possible. I am certain you are going to enjoy our book.

Paul D. Combs
Headmaster, Boston School International
Panama
2016

"I don't know if you've ever noticed this, but first impressions are often entirely wrong... Your initial opinion on just about anything may change over time."
— Lemony Snicket, *The Bad Beginning or, Orphans!* (A Series of Unfortunate Events No. 1)

# A Word From Our Primary Coordinator
## Madelyn Moreno

Teaching owns limitless learning. Educators have the main goal to shape children for their future. Our purpose is to appreciate their needs first. We empathize with our students´ feelings and behaviors and develop enthusiasm and commitment.

The Industrial Age prepared students for "know what and do it." Now the Knowledge Age plans a system based on students' empowerment, not micromanagement. Because of it, we, as leaders, leave behind our comfort zone and consider seriously the role and contribution in each and every student's success, over all difficulties based on their skills, competence, attitudes, attributes, and actions.

Educators explore the potential of each individual student, so he/she can discover his/her own place in a complex and ever shifting present and future world/universe.

If we want to create a sustainable future, we need to discover and nurture the next technologically-savvy generation.

Special Acknowledgment
to my wife
Alicia Frank Haviland,
proofreader extraordinaire, who also
cooked muy rico (very rich) meals
during the plethora of nights, after school,
over the two months time
I edited this book, a labor of love;
me sometimes dozing off at
my laptop after
a very long, joyful school day/week!
(*Not* a run-on sentence!)

# Contents

*In the Future Sci-Fi (Grade 5)*

*My Life in Haiku (Grade 1.1)*
## Foreword by Teacher Elsie Soto

Being a first grade teacher has been a rewarding experience, full of challenges, learning, and affection.

I am very proud of each one of my students and their achievements, skills, and abilities.

I believe they will all be great in the years ahead.

The following is a sample of their writing done while in my first grade classroom. They are quite proud of their writing and want to share it with their families, friends, and the big wide world of readers and writers that exist in and outside their school.

Thank you for taking time to read this wonderful book of writing, not just from my first graders, but from all the other primary students here at Boston School that put pen/pencil to paper.

I like ships a lot
My friend has a lot of ships
I have ships at home

Flowers in my house
Water, sunlight, oxygen
Flower has pollen

I have the Legos
Lots of fun playing with them
I build the cities

I like Nerf a lot
I play with my Nerf a lot
I have a new Nerf

I like my classroom
Playing with my friends at school
I like stories too

I have a cute dog
My dog is smaller than me
I am in the school


I like roses best
The rose lives in my garden
I like to smell it


Look, a teddy owl
I bought it at Albrook Mall
And he loves letters


See the butterfly
The butterfly can fly high
I can play with it


You can eat ice cream
I love vanilla ice cream
Let's go get ice cream

The dog is running
The dog is eating his food
My dog's name is Blue


Flowers grow in dirt
Look at the sky; there is rain
Helps flowers to grow


I like football class
I play football with my mom
We always have fun


I am in my house
I am out in the open
Mom, thanks for coming


Look at teddy bear
I will be naming it Bob
Now he is at home

My fish is orange
I love eating pizza most
Horses eat carrots


My dog is funny
What is his name? It is Cheys
He is color brown


I see a big shark
The shark eats so many fish
The shark can swim fast


The tiger runs fast
Look a tiger in the zoo
He is eating meat


I like dinosaurs
They are big with long brown tails
Oh! A dinosaur

I shop with my mom
I like my dog and my cat
My dad is with me


The dog eating food
I know his name is Cacho
He is running fast


I see blue flowers
Bee likes the blue flowers here
Takes pollen from them


I like my teacher
She helps me to learn letters
School is so much fun


Spaghetti is good
With red sauce, noodles, and cheese
Very delicious

I love my mommy
She bakes cheese pizza for me
Now, eat some pizza


The rainbow is nice
Rainbow has lots of colors
I really like it


She is beautiful
My favorite dog, Dora
Likes to play with me


Flowers smell so good
Flowers are so beautiful
I do like flowers


The raindrops come down
I watch from my house window
So many wet drops

Cool light laser here
My bag is half full of toys
The bag is so big


The flower is big
Flowers have many colors
Flowers need water


My horse runs so fast
He can run ten miles per day
I like my new horse


The tiger is cool
A tiger is in the zoo
Is orange and black


The jungle is there
Want to go to the jungle
A monkey is there

I like flowers and
The smell of flowers is nice
They need water too


Woody is a toy
From the Toy Story movie
Buzz Lightyear is too


The T-Rex is big
It is a green dinosaur
Roar! Help! Here it comes


I like Iron Man
He is a super hero
Iron man can fly


Star Wars is scary
Luke Skywalker's a Jedi
The Star Wars is cool

Elephant is big
It likes eating and sleeping
I love elephants


My zebra runs fast
Marty is my zebra's name
My little zebra


I see a flower
We need plants to live on Earth
I do love flowers


I do like my clothes
My clothes are pink and purple
They are to try out


Look! My butterfly
My butterfly can fly up
Her name is Alice

I have a big dog
He's a boy named Pepita
He kisses my face


Flowers need water
Flowers are so beautiful
Flowers smell so good


I have a best friend
Anelisse and I have fun
Her name is lovely


The rainbow is nice
I love all my family
I like the rainbow


Nicole is my friend
I play with her at her house
I have a good time

I have new Tazos
They are from the Dragon Ball
A hero, Goku


Wow, Star Wars movie
Look, Darth Vader is coming
There comes the Star Ship


Sunset is here now
That means the day will be done
Red, orange, yellow


I have a sister
She is bigger than I am
She is in sixth grade


Scooby Doo I watch
It's the best show on TV
A dog that's so cool!

*My Life in Haiku (Grade 1.2)*
## Foreword by Teacher Mindy Cooper

What do I like most about teaching 1st grade? It's that my students are ready and happy to learn everything. They give me the energy to do great and fun things each and every day.

What my students will take away from this book writing project is that they had a "blast" and enjoyed writing in a whole new way, especially with Teacher Joe teaching them so enthusiastically. Using haiku, the Japanese art of poetry, they learned how to express themselves better and to improve their writing significantly.

Also, they were required to count syllables, 5, 7, 5, so it had cross-curricular application to math.

I can honestly say that this has been my greatest homeroom class ever in an educational career that has spanned seven years now.

Here's two haiku (Hey, that rhymes!) to prove it!


We have fun learning
Glue, clay, colors, numbers, shapes
It's a first grade thing


We dance and we play
We add and take away. Yay!
So, have a great day

The dog is big, cool
My dog is big and can jump
My dog can swim, splash

A big dinosaur
And I have a little toy
Dinosaur eats food

The car can go fast
I see a car on the road
The car is dark black

Going to the park
At the park I see two friends
I play with my friends

I go to the pool
You cannot run at the pool
At the pool I swim

## Dario Garcia Gallardo

I love my red cap
My cap also has orange
My cap is Burpi


I go to the beach
I like to help clean the beach
Happy at the beach


I see a green frog
She can jump very high up
I love my green frog


I have a brown bear
It is a soft teddy bear
I love that brown bear


I love red markers
I make things with the markers
My marker is cool

All my friends and me
We go to school every day
She sits in our class

My dog is happy
My dog is in the green park
He plays with a cat

The cat is sleepy
The cats play at the cat park
And the park is big

I love my cute dog
Happy are my mom and dog
The cat is so sad

I go to the pool
Oh! The cat is in the pool
I jump in the pool

My friends are in school
We are playing at recess
Look! A butterfly


I play with my friend
Clarissa is my friend's name
I love Clarissa


Shoelaces are long
I like my white shoelaces
They go on my feet


I go to the park
I see my friend Camila
I play with my friend


I see the plant grow
I love the plant, beautiful
The plant grows up, up

There's one of my friends
Friends play at recess time here
See people jumping


One of the circles
A girl looks at the flower
It grows and grows more


I have a pink owl
Her name is Princess Lila
Lila loves to play


Playing in my room
I see my toy Sparkles there
I was so happy


My lunch bag is cool
The lunch bag is all for me
I will eat my lunch

Spiderman went out
And he smelled it too much then
He doesn't see it


I see a T-Rex
There are two dinosaurs here
They go in a cave


I go exploring
For something so very cool
What I find? Not cool


I go to my school
Then I go to my house fast
Then I need to sleep


I go to the park
It is going to rain out
We had to leave fast

The plants grow up fast
All of them are different
And they can be wet


I do like cool bears
She is just called Blanca Bit
She is six years old


A girl has a cake
The cupcake is colorful
The girl eats it. Yum!


The bear plants a plant
The cat has a cute white dress
The mouse eats small cheese


My pet can jump high
When it is tired it sleeps
When it sleeps it snores

Mom gave me a cat
Then it goes and slips in tub
My cat goes to house


I see a pink shoe
I want to buy the pink shoes
Pink is my color


I love the giraffe
I have a nice sweet giraffe
I love my giraffe


Like to ride a bike
My bike's color is yellow
It is so pretty


One day at the park
It was great to run and play
At my house I sleep

Once upon a time
It was the first day of school
I like my teacher


My friend, me are here
We are doing our classwork
She and I at school


They are very nice
I like to play with my friends
I do like my friends


We go to the park
That is where we play all day
But not on school days


I like my best friend
I play with my new best friend
You are my best friend

The hen is with chicks
The chickens play with my mom
Time to eat the chicks


I'm Luke Skywalker
I get into a big plane
Then fly into space


Angry Birds, Star Wars
Skywalker plays with his friends
I play with my friends


T-Rex is funny
The T-Rex needs more water
He likes to play too


Luke Skywalker sees
Darth Vader, then runs to him
I draw his airplane

A girl with friends here
They don't like to take a bath
And they all smell, Eew

School is cool and fun
Boston International
I do my homework

I like the colors
My favorite color? Pink
I have a rainbow

I am a princess
I have one pet; it's a cat
I have a big dress

I like my big bow
The bow is soft and light pink
Beautiful big bow

# Gabriel Andres Vergara Flores

I see a white shark
This shark was a dinosaur
The shark went to sleep


Play with my brother
"Catch is fun," my brother said
And we go to sleep


My teacher is fun
I go to school and have fun
Love my super school


I bake a big cake
My brother eats the cake too
It tastes very good


I play with my pup
My puppy runs really fast
My dog wins the race

*The End in Mind*

Through the years I have learned to appreciate the unique opportunity to serve a higher purpose, as it is, to make a difference in the lives of small children.

Sharing (because that is what we do day by day. We share, learn, enjoy, feel, and grow together) with students from elementary, allows me to help them to feel proud to live following moral values.

We teach them to respect others' ways of thinking when we give possible solutions and ideas about ways to solve a given situation in class (they learn tools to apply when they are by themselves).

As teachers, we have learned how to teach the importance of inquiry and how to make decisions and set goals.

Through writing, our students have learned to discover and explore the magical power of their creative minds. They approach their works saying, "Teacher, but it's too difficult," but little by little, as they keep trying, images and ideas come to their minds and they show me their works and tell me what is going to happen next.

I ask them questions and share ideas, suddenly they smile and say, "I know what is going to happen next." It is all so very rewarding.

This work, *More or Less/Más o Menos* has given them a chance to prove themselves. And it is in the same spirit that our students at BSI give their best in everything they do.

As our recently passed beloved Director, Frederic Gornell

often said in school and life, "Failure is not an option!" I know he'd be very proud of this book and all the students and teachers who synergized to make it possible. We all had an end in mind: publication of our collective writing, which is now this book you hold in your hands. It's a lasting tribute to Dr. Gornell and all those who choose to be educators and share their love of learning for future generations to carry forward.

<u>Rabbit</u>

Is white
Very furry
Is a mammal also
It can really jump very high
Is soft

I am a rabbit named Lucia. My color is white and I have a short tail. I can speak in rabbit talk. I was two years old and eating lettuce with my mother, Daniela, when the I lost her.

There was a tornado but she didn't survive it. I do not have a family now, but I still go to school with all the other animals. The other animals are laughing at me because I am so little. I am three years old now and the others are between 8 and 18 years old.

One day another adult rabbit adopted me. Their names are Carla and Roberto. Carla is 28 years old and Roberto is 40.

And then I have a family. My father gives me food. I live in a house. They wash me.

I told Carla and Roberto all the things that happened to me.

"Oh my gosh," they said and told me how sorry they were for me.

"I think that you are so sad," Carla told me.

I told them, "No, I'm not."

I went with Carla and Roberto to a tree.

The next day we found out that Carla was pregnant. We don't know if it'll be a boy or a girl yet.

When we find out I am jumping for joy knowing that I'll be a sister since it'll be a girl. I can't believe I'm going to have a sister. "Eeeeee!"

So, now I can tell mom that I am going to see my sister, okay. She told me to be careful.

My birthday is on August 20. That means tomorrow is my birthday and I'm going to be the oldest sister.

Snake

Is fast
The snake is fun
They like to move their tail
It moves when it decides to strike
They bite

I am a snake and my name is Messi. I like ice cream. I am a baby snake and I sometimes attack people, but then I went to the park and found out that nobody liked to play with me in the park.

Then I found a snake and his name is Ronaldo.

"Hello," I said to him. "Do you want to play?"

Ronaldo answered yes, but then told me that he was hungry. So, the two of us went to eat a hamburger.

I liked the hamburger so much that Ronaldo bought me twenty hamburgers, but then he didn't have much money left to buy another hamburger for himself so I shared a few of mine with him.

I said to Ronaldo, "You know that we don't have legs and we are both carnivores?"

"Yes, I know that," Ronaldo answered, and then said something about snakes being covered with overlapping scales and how there are many species of us out there in the world.

That's when I found my family and said goodbye to Ronaldo.

<u>Cat</u>

Four legs
I have a nose
The cat likes to run fast
I have a soft, furry body
Meow!

I was a house cat that weighed about 9 lbs in a family of cats and I could do many things. I was happy. But then the brother cat wanted to fight and I began to run and run.

Then I met a kitten without a family and no food and I get food for the kitten and the family I lived with adopted him and so he was happy.

But then one day a man came to help the kitten, who liked to run and run. It was scary being alone again because the kitten was lost. Soon the kitten was found by another family with cats, and they were friends of mine.

One of those cats saw the kitten and said, "I am your sister, Carla. Let's play."

The kitten said, "Okay, let's play."

But then Carla was lost and the kitten didn't know what to do. That's when he and I went to look for Carla.

We needed to find out where Carla was and we did. That's when she told me that she is my sister too. So we were all happy again. And we run, run, run.

I said, "I can't believe it."

"What can't you believe?"

"That you're my sister too."

<u>Fox</u>

Is big
Fox has four legs
I am orange and white
I am a mammal and drink milk
Run fast


I am the color orange and white; my eyes are black. I am a fox. I live with my family. My favorite food is grass. My name is Kate and I live in the tundra.

The families of the fox have a difficult time talking because one day the fox of winter and the fox of the summer fought.

I have a sister and her name is Diamond and she is liked by the foxes of both winter and summer.

My father is like a wolf and a dog all together. We all belong to the canine family. Out of 39 species there are only 12 real species of foxes and we can be found all around the world in forests, grasslands, and mountains.

I was walking like a fox in the grass when I met a boy named Huntry. He was a friend of mine. He was with his friends and I was with my sister. There was another boy named Fernand and he's an omega. We all played together until it was time to go home.

<u>Wolf</u>

Sharp teeth
Likes to hunt pig
Eats a lot of meat too
The wolf is strong and very fast
Is black

I am a wolf and I like to eat meat because I have very sharp teeth. Of course you know that wolves are mammals. I am a predator who eats sheep, pigs, and sometimes people. My name is Mick, the wolf.

I am not a person. One day I see another wolf just like me. "You can be my friend," I said to her. Gerldan agreed.

"I have three babes. One is Meesil, the other is Nemar, and the third is Suarez. The three cubs are growing in a den and their dad is set to go to Germany."

When I followed Gerldan to the den, I found three wolf cubs housed in a big den in a big bed. They had just seen a bear.

<u>Buzz</u>

Bumble
Bee, black/yellow
Likes to eat much honey
It has six legs and can fly high
Two wings

One day I woke up with my hands and feet in the flower and I wanted to try honey. I loved it. Don't all bees? Then I went off flying to look for some more. Then a human started bothering me. I wanted to sting that human but I didn't because I knew I would die.

Instead, I flew away and some yellow dust stuck to me. I stopped to talk with some bees to ask them what it was; they told me that it was called, pollen.

That's when I went to eat some honey. At the same time a bear wanted to eat my honey so I went away. I had very many friends who also lived in the top of a flower with a lot of honey.

I buzzed around a garden and saw 250 different types of bumblebees. And I used my sense of smell to detect flowers rich in nectar. Do you know that my sense of smell is located on the antennas on the top of my head?

I like to eat the nectar collected from various flowers. We bees are divided into three groups: queen, work bees and drones.

My favorite is the queen bee because she lays eggs so there are more bees in the world.

There was a frog that wanted to eat me but I wouldn't let him.

My body is covered with tiny, tiny hairs. I won't grow that

big, reaching three to four inches in length. My body is also with alternating colors, yellow and black.

I have a lot of bumblebee friends. We can all survive in different habitats and altitudes. We have a lot of fun together.

<u>Whale</u>

Orca
Assassin whale
I am a sea mammal
I have black and white everywhere
Am fast

Once upon a time I was sleeping and when I woke up I was in the ocean swimming. I am an Orca whale and I am black and white. My name is Black and White. I eat fish. But I don't like shark. I am a part of the dolphin family. I am so big that even if I tried now I could not get back into my house where I used to live as a human girl.

I have a sister Orca and her name is Abcd. One day we both saw a dolphin. We also found a fish and a shark.

I want to be human again, but I can't do it. I now see fish all the time, like sharks and dolphins. I also see lots of boats. Now I act as if I was born in the water and have always been here. But that doesn't stop me from thinking about where I used to live and I want to be in my old house. I beg for that an say, "Aaaaah!" I am so mad about this that I want to scream. The other fish would ask, "What are you doing?"

Abcd said, "You're crazy. What are you doing?"

I told her, "I am so confused. Maybe I am crazy!"

"You are crazy," Abcd agreed, which I didn't like very much.

"I love ballet and gymnastics and those are things I can't do because I'm a whale."

I also didn't have an Orca mother, nor did Abcd. We were orphans. I wondered how I ended up with the name Black and White. And how did my sister end up with the name "Abcd?"

I continued speaking to Abcd. "I know my human family is waiting for me. And I'm stuck here. What am I going to do? I'm now living in the ocean. I swim all day just like you."

Abcd didn't know what to say.

The next day I found my human family swimming in the water at the beach. They had a new pet and it was a penguin. That was a problem because now I not only eat fish, but I eat penguins too.

I was confused. I wanted to eat the penguin, but it was my family's pet. And so I just went away. I see another Orca; it was so big.

I shouted, "Abcd, look! I see someone there. Come with me."

Abcd told me, "I think I saw it."

That day in our house, Abcd said, "It's our mother."

I had never seen my mother for real. I was so happy but I kept thinking all about my human family. I was no longer an orphan.

I am a killer whale and I live in Alaska. I am a mammal. I could eat twenty people at one time, but I don't like to do that. I eat lots of fish instead.

I am the biggest of my family. Dolphins are intelligent like me. Humans think that we are just fish but they are crazy. We are mammals like them.

My family is called Delphinidae. We're also called whale calves and even adult whales.

I go with my mother to eat pizza, sushi, hamburgers and ice cream with my hands; sorry, I mean my mouth.

I asked my mother, "Is my name Black and White and my sister's name is Abcd?"

She answered, "No, your name is Clara and your sister's name is Nicole."

### Crocodile

Like fish
I have sharp teeth
I am a big reptile
The crocodile has a long tail
Am brown

I am a crocodile with very sharp teeth. I live in the water and love to eat meat of any kind. I love to swim. Scientist call me a reptile. Besides sharp teeth, I also have sharp claws. When I get old enough I will lay eggs and have crocodiles of my own.

A crocodile has strong muscles in the tail. Sometimes the crocodile is in the sunlight and sometimes in the water with its mouth open. Where there is sunlight it's a good time to catch prey in the border of the river.

Did you know that crocodiles vary in size? The biggest ones live in salt water, like me, and can grow to 13-18 feet and weigh as much as 2,200 pounds. There are dwarf crocodiles and they are only five feet in length and weigh about 40-70 pounds.

<u>Komodo</u>

Dragon
I have four legs
I am green and black too
My prey can't escape my strong bite
Reptile

On the Indonesian islands of Komodo, I am one of 3,000 dragons still alive. I'm a giant reptile who is a descendant from very large varanid lizards that lived across Indonesia and Australia and that died out after the Pleistocene age more than 3.8 million years ago.

Sometimes I think I am a fearful beast. That's really just a wish, a dream. I think of the many animals there are in the world like lions, gorillas, anacondas in the Amazon River and so many others. But when I imagine I am a dragon of Komodo, it beats them all. With my terrible set of teeth and strong jaws my bite leaves no way of escape for my prey.

As a small lizard, I like to climb up trees with my powerful feet. I swim quickly and I love to live close to the water where I dig holes in the ground. I enjoy living along or wandering in small groups with my friends. People call me a land crocodile but I am more like an alligator.

Know why I'm important? Because I can clean the land from dead animal bodies. But I also can eat live animals. If I bite an animal it will surely die not just because of my teeth but also the poisonous bite packed with deadly bacteria.

I will grow to about three meters and weigh about 70 kilograms.

<u>Horse</u>

Gallops
I have four legs
The horse likes to eat grass
I am a very big mammal
Am white

One day I dreamed of being a horse and the next day I woke up I was a brown horse. I have a tail and run very fast. I can also talk.

The first day of school I woke up very early in the morning. I went running to school. I love my teacher, who is also a horse. I also love my friends, all of whom are horses too; they are the best. But each one goes, "blah, blah, blah," which is the way my friends and I talk as horses.

Then you might say, "Stop! No way." But, it's true.

Now I have to tell you that all my friends were suddenly mad at him. Why?

Because our teacher shouted, "Get out!"

Wup!

Then it's the end of school and the bus picks me up, and I go home. This time not running.

They tell me we are going to the veterinarian. Yaky. She's a dog. Wow! A dog is a veterinarian. "Impossible," you say?

Yaky told me, "You are a warmblooded animal, developed-between crosses of other horses."

The next day I see another horse just like me, named Cristale.

"I am your sister," she says to me.

"I will tell you that your class of horse is mammalian."

She asked me, "Are we wild horses?"

I told her, "Yes we are."

### Koala Bear

Am gray
I eat a lot
I have a big brown nose
Koalas are bears with big eyes
Slowly

One day I was so surprised when I became a koala bear. I am now a girl koala, of course. And I eat a lot of ice cream and I don't have that many teeth. I have an older sister and her name is Dawn. My name is Eve.

We don't have a family but that never stops us. We both go to school every day and we still have recess like when I was a human being.

I am an orphan now and my sister is also one.

Three months later, when school is out for summer, we go on a trip to find our mother. That's when we find our Koala family.

Then five years later it is the first day of school for that year.

When I arrive at school the teacher tells the little animals there to "present yourselves."

As one of the students, I tell the class that I am herbivorous and that "I like to eat eucalyptus leaves, 500 grams daily. I also don't usually have to drink water because the leaves I eat give me lots of water. I will also eat the leaves from tea and cherry trees." I also explain that *koala* in the language of the Aborigines, native to Australia, means "who do not drink." The class loves me and my presentation.

Then, two hours later, I meet a tiger. Her name is Kate and she is six years old like me. Then we go out to play.

<u>Dolphin</u>

Bigger
I drink the milk
The dolphin swims in pool
I am gray and intelligent
I jump

I am a dolphin and I am drinking milk. I am swimming with my friend and I am so happy. I have five brothers. I am so happy living in the water. We sometimes play Tic-tac-toe. Now I am in school. I have a test in grammar. I finished the test and the school day passes quickly. Now I am going to bed.

Today is the day I think is my birthday. I am going to Camp Wood. Oh no, I get lost. What do I do? The woods are scary. I want to go home

"Aaaaaah! Help me, help me?" Then someone did help me.

"Oh thanks sir, you saved me."

The man asked, "What happened, did the wolf attack you?"

"Yes," I answered.

"Weren't you a dolphin anyway?"

I didn't know how to answer that. All I knew was that I was scared.

### Anteater

So cool
Nose is too long
I have very long legs
The anteater moves so slowly
Licks ants

One day I changed into an anteater and there were so many other anteaters who were talking to me. That's right, talking to me, in English. Can you believe that? We like playing together. I have so many friends.

One minute I was a boy and the next I woke up and I was living as an anteater.

I go to school with other anteaters and we play a lot and even have recess like I did when I was human. After school we went to the park. We passed a cool football soccer field and ended up playing football and basketball.

Then one day I was sick and I went to see the doctor and he said I had gastritis. Do you know what that is?

As an anteater I am a very funny looking creature. I can eat many ants, something like 30,000. I am so slow. I have a long tongue that is two feet long. I grow to be seven feet long.

Then I am cured of gastritis. Many days pass and I went to school and saw some new anteater friends.

<u>Dog</u>

Runs fast
Am a mammal
Lives inside a house here
I eat dog food and wag my tail
Brown dog

I am a dog. My name is Zoey. I have black fur. I like to play and sleep. I'm a mammal. I live in a house with a human. I am big. I have four legs. I eat bones. I have lots of friends who have brown and white fur. Many say I look like a wolf and I like that. My eyes are black and I am just a puppy who's a Labrador. My best friend is also a puppy and her name is Miranda. We both like to go and play at the park where we run every day.

<u>Panda Bear</u>

Panda
I have sharp teeth
Pandas get in the trees
Pandas eat a lot of bamboo
So cute

I am a a panda. Do you think pandas go to school? No!
I spend most of my day eating all the bamboo I want. I
have sharp teeth and I am a herbivore. As a panda, I live on a
mountain in the forest.
The man said, "You can go to mountain in two days."
I thank him and move on.
As a panda, I like to go to quiet places.
We take care of our babies and give everything to them.

Puffer Fish

Inflates
I have sharp spikes
Puffer eats other fish
Puffer fish is not a small fish
Am brown

One day I was suddenly a puffer fish. My name is Spinfish. My friends tell me that I "talk too much." But that doesn't matter because every day they want to play with me.

The name of my puffer fish friends are Hanna and Juan. They are very friendly, of course. Some days we swim in other parts of the ocean with the permission of our parents. And we love to eat algae.

On Monday the school week starts up again. Even as fish we still go to school. We swim in schools of fish; that's where one Orca named Cristaline said, "Hello."

I greeted the Orca. "Hi. My name is Spinfish."

"See you tomorrow," said Cristaline, who I found out was eight years old. I am fifteen.

"See you tomorrow," she responded in English.

Then it was time to sleep. I slept standing up.

In the morning, my mom said, "Spinfish, today is day of the princess and you have to dress like your favorite princess, while boys look like their favorite knights."

I told my mom all about Cristaline and then I went to the scientific school where I learned all about puffer fish. My classmates and I sat at our desks and the teacher told us that there are different species of porcupine fish of which puffer fish belong.

"What do you think of that, Spinfish?" the teacher asked.

"Wow!" That's all I could say.

And then our teacher said, "Puffer fish vary in size from one inch long, called pygmy puffer, to a foot long."

I already knew that sharks are the only species who can't die from puffer fish's toxin.

That's when it was time to eat. At our school we go home for lunch. I went home and asked my mom if I could visit Cristaline. She said yes.

So, I went to see Cristaline, who was with her own mother.

I said, "Hello."

At first she didn't listen to me.

I had to scream, "HELLO!"

That's when she listened to me.

And we talked.

Butterfly

Gorgeous
Colorful light
Miracle of nature
Caterpillar, then Butterfly
Fly, Fly

With this book project I believe my class was exposed to thinking, inquiring, putting their thoughts in order so they could express themselves in writing. They learned how to write a cinquain and a short story. They accessed their imagination beautifully. In their writing they used vocabulary like predator, mammal, herbivore, and carnivore that they had already learned in class.

Like the paper butterflies hanging from our classroom ceiling, my 2nd graders all took flight in their writing.

I found out that it is possible for my students to write a published book when everyone synergizes in a proactive manner. We all worked individually and then as a group to fulfill our book and prove that dreams do come true.

Helping my students to express themselves creatively and share this learning experience with others is an experience I will never forget.

What I like most about teaching 2nd graders is that I get to help these little ones mature academically and see how quickly they grow up.

They are the future and my teaching now will make a difference later.

<u>Stripes</u>

Zebra
Black and white stripes
Running, jumping, pacing
A picture, a wonderful sight
I'm free

I am a zebra, which is a mammal. As a zebra, I don't lay any eggs. I am like a horse and part of that family. I can tell when my predators are close. I have very good hearing. I can also see things far away. I love to run, as fast as 35 miles per hour. This way I can try to escape danger.

I like to protect the herd. I'm always at the back of the group to defend against other animals.

My stripes are like your human fingerprints. Each zebra's stripes are different.

I like to bray. Have you heard me bray before? When I bray, my friends can hear me. I can also make snorting sounds. Can you believe that I can "talk" to other zebras with my eyes and ears?

Being a zebra is cool! Don't you think?

<u>Gold Fish</u>

I swim
I love gold fish
The gold fish has no feet
The gold fish is not small or big
Gold fish

One day I became a little gold fish named Nemo. That day I said, "Let's go to school." I looked for my mom but couldn't find her. My brother Allie knew I was in school. I like to play and swim. Of course I live in water where I eat plants every day. I also lay eggs in the water.

I like pizza. My friends are Aliza, Gabriel, David, Valeria, Dori, and Alan. I went to see Dori and she said, "What do you need?"

I told her that I needed some food.

Allie came to Dori's house and asked, "What are you doing?"

"I am eating pizza," Dori answered. "By the way, where's Nemo?"

Allie said she didn't know.

A search for me began. First, Allie asked Aliza if she saw Nemo.

Aliza answered, "Yes, I saw Nemo going to school."

So, Allie swam to my school to talk to me.

"Why are you here?" Allie asked when she found me in the playground.

"Why aren't you at school?" I asked Allie. "Are you being punished? Were you expelled?"

"They can't punish Allie," Gabriel said. "It's not fair." Then he added, "I am from China."

"Why are you so red?" I asked Allie.

"Because I am sick," said Allie. "But maybe David can help me."

But David said, "I can't help you right now."

"Why not?"

"I can't tell you now." Then David asked, "Aliza, why are you so lazy?"

<u>Horse</u>

I run
The horse runs fast
Horses live on a farm
They are man's best and loyal friends
Love them

I suddenly became a horse with a colorfully spotted coat. I found out that horse breeds are divided into three categories: hot bloods, warm bloods, and cold bloods.

Hot bloods are very spirited and have speed and endurance. They are used for racing, like the Anglo Arabians.

Cold bloods are draft or farm horses, and warm bloods are like a Clydesdale.

And warm bloods, which I am one, is a cross between cold bloods and hot bloods. I might even be an Appaloosa, with a thin mane and tail. Some believe that my eyes have an almost human look to them. I can believe that, as I once was a boy!

All I know for sure is that I like to run and run all the time.

## Sea Turtle

Swim good
I have a shell
I live in the ocean
I love the sea turtles so much
Do you?

One day I was swimming in the sea. I love to play. But now I'm swimming in a school of sea turtles. I really love to swim and I was searching for my mom, who I love so much. That's why I went to find her.

My name is Seaturtt.

One day I was at school and I saw my friends Dori, a blue fish, Luchi, an octopus, and Nemo, a goldfish.

Then I went to talk with my teacher and my teacher said, "You have a good grade. Did you know that?"

You probably know that I live in the ocean. Turtles have been around for more than 220 million years. I live in the beaches where I was born. I lay eggs in the holes of the sand. Some of my other family members can weigh as much as 1,000 pounds. My little brother is hatching and it's taking all day long. I don't have teeth. I can go anywhere, like 12,000 miles from Indonesia to Oregon.

<u>Rabbit</u>

Food chain
I want to jump
Tiger wants to eat me
I need to hop into my hutch
Be safe

I am a rabbit, a mammal, and I live in a den and I like to hop. I don't like to get dirty because then I have to take a bath, but I like that anyway.

Then I go to my house and my mom is there. She tells me I have to take a bath and I say to my mom, "I don't like baths."

And then I go to school. I see my friends and they are gossiping. And the teacher says, "You have a bad grade and I am furious."

After that we go to lunch. When school is over we go to my house and I start chopping with my mom. When we're chopping, I saw my father and it was great.

Then the other day I found out that I am an enemy of the carnivores. So that's when I no longer like what I am.

<u>Bear</u>

I growl
I love my cub
A bear is really big
The rain forest has many bears
The bear

I see a bear on its hind legs. I am a bear too. I find out that bears like honey. I can't lay any eggs because I'm a mammal. I have fingernails. I have a million friends in the forest.

One day I eat a live fish right out of the river.

My friend's name is Santiago. Both he and I had to sleep in a hollow tree. We like to rub up against trees and even bite trees to let other bears and animals know that is our home.

Tiger

Mammal
With lots of stripes
The king of the forest
The tiger is a carnivore
Roar, roar

I am a tiger and I like to eat meat. I am a mammal. I have hair and fur. I hide in the tall grass because the animals can't see me because I am the same color as the grass.

I run fast and I eat other animals. I like to sleep. I am dangerous and have long teeth and big eyes.

I have a special family that I live with.

The king of the forest is what I am.

As a tiger I am so dangerous because tigers can eat your brain.

As a tiger I am best known for my stripes. I am a solitary animal, which means I like to be alone. I have large paws that are sharp with retractable claws.

<u>Octopus</u>

Showy
Cool movement too
I have eight legs, three hearts
A blue blooded invertebrate
Octi

I am in my house eating eggs. I have eight legs. I have to go to my school. I have a big bag and my pen and notebook and my book. I'm a big, beautiful Octopus.

Did you know that I love to eat algae with salt water? I don't need a plate to put my food on because I have eight arms. That's true. But something I don't like is that I don't have a mom and I was six years old when I lost her. Now I am ten years old. Just two days ago I saw a red octopus.

It looked like me!

It was my mom but she did not see me. I was so angry, but do you know something? I don't like that I don't have a sweater and I'm so cold.

I saw a little piece of leaf and under it I saw a bottle and a box, I opened it and it was soda and pizza. Yes it was! Now I'm not sad. I'm so happy.

Well, I was in school with my 105 friends and my turtle teacher. My name is Luchi and my best friends are Seaturtt and Pucee. I love them.

My head is located in my mantle. My blood is blue. I can even change my color. I have 148,000 sisters and one brother. I am now blue and I love this color, but soon I'll be yellow.

Lion

Tall grass
I catch zebras
Lions run in tall grass
Big lions are so dangerous
Roar, roar

One day I was trying to catch a zebra when I saw one hundred zebras. I am a lion.

That's when I caught five zebras and my family and I ate them. Next the little ones go to the lion school. I said, "roar" that means "go to school."

Then we were all lying in the tall grass. We saw another big zebra. We caught it and the little ones ate it and said, "roar." That means "thank you."

Then we get to prepare all to play the last game of the day. At night the little ones sleep after eating dinner. The next day the little ones go to school and I walk in the tall grass and find my friend.

In school, the teacher teaches the kids a lot about roars. They were practicing how to catch animals with robots. I was with my friend when lunch was prepared. I said goodbye and went to lunch.

Some days later I started to teach how to vocalize a little at a time. I wanted their roar to be heard five miles away. I like to eat antelopes and zebras, but my favorite food is wildebeests

Lions like me live in the southern and eastern parts of Africa. I choose to live in the south.

I once ate a lunch that was 40 pounds of wildebeest meat.

I love being a lion and that's what I now do in my life.

### Penguin

Black, white
I like the cold
I swim very swiftly
I like to eat fish in the sea
Swim, swim

OMG, I am now living in the Arctic. I am in an egg. I have flippers and a beak. I am a penguin. I don't like being in an egg but I have to. I like to eat fish. It's cool. I am a fast swimmer.

Suddenly I find myself living in a zoo. I went there to find my family. I swam from the Arctic and found them living in this zoo in North America.

But when I got there, they had moved them to Australia. Now I have to buy an airplane ticket. Oh no!

Well, I have no choice. I needed energy so I bought a pizza. I loved it. I bought a whole pizza plane. Ha, ha! And a human ate my plane!

I had to get another plane and we flew that to Africa. That was a vacation after I finished 2nd grade. When I came back for 3rd grade I met a friend called Kvele.

I can't fly so I went on a journey to visit the house of the magical witches in Asia.

I wanted to buy a super pizza. I flew, but my soda power ran out. I stopped in New Zealand. I had to go the penguin store. They wouldn't let me go in. It was night so I needed to wait. So, I told a story about how I could breath underwater for 20 minutes at a time. Wow! And I communicated by making sounds.

Then I fell asleep. It was morning when I woke up and went

again to the penguin store. This time it was open. I bought personal clothes and a new soda power kit. Now I could fly back home and be happy.

I don't really like being in the cold, so that's when I fly to Africa using my soda power.

I met an elephant friend. I saved him from a tiger, who got wet with cold water, so he will never mess with my friends ever again.

Carnivore

Saber
Tooth Tiger me
I am eating my prey
I like sleeping in the forest
Grrr, grrr

I am now living as a saber tooth tiger. Imagine that. I get to kill my prey with just one bite. I have long teeth and am very dangerous. I don't like waking up and I think how cool I am now. I don't talk like humans do, but I go, "Grrr, grrr, grrr."

I also like eating pizza with tomato and cheese. But I am a carnivore.

I hunt other animals who are my prey. I kill them if I want because I need to eat. That's what mammals like me do. Most days I just wander the jungle. Sad but the saber tooth tiger is extinct (around 10,000 B.C.)except for me. I am one of the best known prehistorical animals. I have very large canines sticking out of my mouth and they can be more than 7 inches in size. I am not a relative of the modern day tiger.

I like to roam across the grasslands and plains and open woodlands throughout North and South America, where I live now.

<u>Monkey</u>

I swing
In the jungle
The monkey can swing fast
I can travel through the jungle
Monkeys

When I woke up today I found myself in the jungle. I was swinging in the jungle. I am a monkey.

I don't like swinging in the jungle because then I'm going to get dirty.

My color is brown. I am a mammal, so I don't lay eggs. I like eating bananas.

Do you know that monkeys help each other groom? We help each other get rid of parasites, leaves, and dead skin. That's how we stay healthy. I help my baby with grooming every day.

One more thing. Did you know that that monkey and apes are primates?

<u>Labrador</u>

I walk
I am a dog
I also am running
I live in the house with my friends
I run

I am a dog, a Labrador. I have four legs. I am black. I really like to walk. I have two puppies. One is a girl and the other is a boy. I am a mammal. I live in a house.

Did you know that a group of offspring is called a litter? The father of a litter is called the sire and the mother is called a dame. You know all about puppies, but did you know that when a puppy is born it's called whelping, from Old English word, whelp.

The dogs are called by a fancy name Canis lupus familiaris. The list of dog-like carnivores include the domestic, house dog, wolves, foxes, and jackals.

Today I am going to the park with my own pups. I don't know where my mom is but I love her.

<u>Snake</u>

Slither
I like the snake
She crawls and hugs its eggs
My snake is very beautiful
Beware

One day I woke up as a snake and slithered along saying, "Mom, mom, mom!"

"Yes, honey."

"Can we go to Sofia's house?"

"Okay, but only if you take a bath,"

"I don't want to take a bath."

"But you need one. And we can't go to Sofia's house if you don't have one. You really need a bath."

"Nooooooo!" I answered.

<u>Bull</u>

Muscle
I am a bull
My home is in a zoo
I live in Canada not Spain
Paws dust

I am a bull. The girls in my family are called cows. My color is blue. I am seven years old. I have lots of muscle and I can be really mean, sometimes. My cousins fight in bullfights in Spain. I don't do that because I live in a house, in a zoo in Canada, and they don't allow bullfighting there.

With my horns I can defend myself against predators, we learned about that in my second grade class when I was here at school.

Want to know how much I weigh? 700 kilograms! Come see me at the zoo in Canada. I like visitors.

Butterfly

I fly
I have six legs
Butterflies are insects
I am a pretty butterfly
Dream soul

One day a butterfly left her eggs on a leaf. One egg hatched, and that was me! I was a caterpillar looking for my mom. I yelled, "Mom, Mom, where are you?" I was lost.

A few days ago, as a caterpillar, I changed into a pupa. After a few months I will become a beautiful butterfly. And then I will still be looking for my mom. I am very tired but I don't quit because I never quit.

Hey! I am a butterfly and I have a life cycle. First, a butterfly lays eggs and then the eggs hatch. It becomes a caterpillar, then a bigger caterpillar, a pupa, and then a beautiful butterfly.

I know there are many kinds of butterflies, but we are all from the classroom of insects called Lepidoptera.

I now have brightly colored wings and make fluttering flight. The group I belong to is part of the large super family Papilionoidae.

I'm extremely boastful about my students this year. Most of them already arrived at third grade knowing how to read, in both Spanish and English, Because of this, it's easier for me to assign projects for them to do in groups. I like this age group because they're already quite capable and I'm just helping them to be better at their writing, reading, and other academic pursuits.

From what I heard from my students, after the writing sessions that Mr. Haviland conducted once a week over a period of a couple months, they really enjoyed writing their short stories, with titles like *The Haircut, I Love Learning, My Best Days in Lebanon, The Sweet Ice Cream, The Dog, Skiing Could be Cool.*

Through our StoryTown (Harcourt) text, we've been reading a lot of the realistic fiction genre this school year, so they already had that modeled to them and I'm sure it made writing their stories a little easier, but still challenging in that they had to put their thoughts down on paper and turn their real life experiences into something that became fictional.

Every step of the way, Mr. Haviland has kept students and teachers informed about our book process. I really appreciated that as a teacher.

While he conducted extra writing classes, I continued to work with my students in grammar and phonics so that they could write even better stories.

My kids are excited now to see their words in print. They've already seen them as part of the evolving manuscript for *More or Less*, but I can only imagine what their response will be when

*More or Less* is in actual book form for them to hold in their hands and see their writing along with the writing of all of their primary peers in one beautiful collection.

I hope you enjoy the writing done by my students. In Spanish: Estoy muy orgulloso = I am very proud! Not just of how they've grown academically as students, but citizens who can write about the world around them and share it with others.

This writing is just one part of that growth. They worked really hard on it and this is an educational experience they will remember forever.

# The Haircut

My haircut was cool and I was like "Oh man, oh man!"
My dad even liked it, as did my mom and sister too.
But, I was angry with my mom who wanted me take a bath right after my haircut. It was going to ruin my haircut.

Then my dad talked to me and said, "It's just a haircut, Julio."

I realized that I didn't have to be angry with my mom. After I finished with my bath I still had the same haircut and I was happy all the next day.

I was so happy I almost exploded and I was going to get pizza, a little hair got on the pizza and I didn't want touch it because it was super, super hot but I had to touch it because I didn't have another choice. So, I ate it and I was happy because I have a chocolate milk shake and it was good. Then I went to my home and got an ice cream and it was so tall.

I said to my mom, "What in the world! What did you do to my ice cream?" She didn't answer, just smiled as I devoured it.

Then I went to my cousin's house and my cousin was angry because I broke his video game and he said, "You're going to see what I'm going to do to you." Then he hit me in the face. I told my aunt and he was grounded. Of course he was even more angry and I went to my house and he was saying, "So! So! So! So! I'm the best cousin in the world."

"Oh thanks Julio, well let's go. Okay?" That's what I said.

Then we were watching a movie and playing a video game.

# I Love Learning

One day it was my first day at school. I worked on math and I said, "Math is the best subject of my life because every type of math that I learn and know better when I grow older. When people tell me about math I will already know it."

I am going to learn how to be an expert in Art because everything you know you had to learn at one time, right?

When I go to university I will learn how to be an expert of Art because everything you learn you will know forever.

I was talking with a friend and I got a 100 and she got a 99 so I told the teacher that I got a 100 and I won the race. But the bad girl told me that she won the super race. I told my mom the truth about the test. Then I went to eat pizza at Pizza Brava and it was my first time at Pizza Brava and then I went to Hollywood, it wasa crazy thing and I was in the pool. So, I said, "Watch it friends!" And I jumped all over them.

So I say "Sorry. Okay?" I kept playing in the pool and then I got out of the pool because I was getting tired and wanted to go to sleep.

Then I thought I was going to math today because I was crazy. I did a lot of math, math, math, math, math. Then I stopped doing math, finally, and I was free forever.

That's when I went to the park with my friend and it was the best day ever.

When I got home I ate and did homework, but there was too much homework. Finally I went to sleep.

The next day I was angry because I didn't want to go to school, but my mom said, "If you don't go to school, you will never learn anything."

So, I told my mom That I already know math and I'm not moving from bed.

"Please, Mom, I don't want to go to school." So I didn't! I stayed at home with my friend, Andrea, who was asking me if I wanted to go to the park. That's where I saw my friend and she pushed me and I didn't like it when she did that to me. I told her mom and she punished her daughter by not letting her go to the park.

This girl never apologized, or said, "I'm sorry."

My bff (best friend forever) and I had a lot of fun together. Meanwhile my mom was sleeping and we were watching TV. That's when Andrea told me that she had an invisible friend.

"Are you crazy?" I asked her.

And she said, no, that "girls can play with invisible friends."

# New Country/New Friends

One day there was a girl named Sara. She loved her school because they only spoke English. Then a new student came to class. She was called Adriana. She always bothered all of the other students. Sara wanted to go home because Adriana bullied her more than the other classmates. She tried to get other people to laugh at Sara.

Two days later, Sara's mother and father put her in a school in Spain. She didn't know anything. Then a girl named Marina taught Sara how to talk Spanish.

"Hola," said Marina. Sara asked herself what she was saying. Sara ran away. Marina didn't know why she ran.

"¿Espera a hablar en español?" asked Marina.

A classmate of Marina, who was bilingual said, "Marina asked you, 'Do you want to speak Spanish?'"

Then Sara told her that she did want to learn Spanish, but right now only spoke English.

Marina understood.

"Hey, I can teach you how to speak Spanish" said Marina. Sara smiled. Then Marina showed Sara how to speak some Spanish. But when Sara went to the classroom, she did not understand.

The teacher presented Sara to the class. She was a little scared because she did not know Spanish. At recess, Marina told Sara to come to a place that no one was using.

"We are going to start class here," said Marina.

Two weeks later she learned everything in Spanish. Then a new student came and she was called Carla. She was a bully and a couple of days later Sara was not happy.

"I am … I better not to tell you my name," said Sara.

Carla was very angry. Sara was too. No, she was just tired of fighting.

Sara went to the cafeteria and bought chicken nuggets. Marina bought a hamburger and fries. That's when Carla showed up and Sara started thinking about what she had done.

Carla said, "Marina is, well, I don't know what to say. She is so bad!"

"You are the BAD girl, not Marina," said Sara, who just sat there, face in her hand. She added, "I wish you had never come to this school."The bell sounded .

"It's time to go home," said Sara to Marina, not looking at Carla.

Sara went to the bus. When Carla passed her she looked at her with a mean face. When it was time for Sara to get off the bus, Carla yelled at her, "Get off the bus."

Later, when she arrived home, Carla's nanny asked, "What happened?"

"Sara made me fall," lied Carla.


Two months later, Carla finally apologized to Sara .

"What? You're now saying you're sorry to me?" Sara was still angry.

"Yes, I think so," said Carla

"Well, I don't accept it." Sara knew Carla hadn't stopped being a bully and she wasn't really sorry.

"Okay. Sorry you don't accept my apology!"

That's when the two girls walked away from each other.

# Skiing Could be Cool

I was having one of my dreams. Suddenly I was skiing down a melting ice mountain. That's when I fell into a dark cave. It was all dark, but not for long. That's when bright lights began to pop-on allowing me to see.

Problem was, I didn't know where to go. There were five paths. I went down the first one where there were more paths and a couple of levers. There were also some holes and I didn't know what they were for. I was trying to push open the door, but it didn't work, so I decided to try the second path.

On the second path there were flying rocks and a golden diamond. I was thinking about the first path where the holes were. So then I put the golden diamond inside the hole and it worked.

So, I was now wondering if the door would open. But then I went to the second path and I saw a blue diamond something. But what was it? A giant wall came from the sky.

"That is weird," I said to myself.

Then it showed like some numbers. So it asked, "What's 9 + 10?"

I said, "21?"

The wall said, "You are correct!"

Well, I got the diamond and put it into the hole. I went on the third path and it didn't have anything weird. Then I saw a light brightening at the end of the hall; it turned out to be a red torch, which got brighter as I approached it.

Like a flying diamond, rocks of little diamonds, and lots of other things were there. I touched the torch and something was trying to appear. I touched it four times and a red diamond appeared. I touched it again and it worked in the first path where the door was. I entered in the path where the door had opened. I said, "Finally! Oh my..." There was like a portal and on a printed card it said, BACK TO REAL LIFE. Then, for just a moment, I realized I was in one of my dreams and I said to myself, "I must get back to real life."

Two years later, I was on my way back there. Then BOOM! I fell into the same cave. I did another 250 days there. So I saw another me doing the same things I did in the cave on the previous visit. So, I said to the cave walls, "If this is the same thing I did in the cave before that means that I..., huh?!"

I concluded that this is the same dream, but if that is not me, then who is it?

That's when Evil Lucas spoke, saying, "Who is there?"

# *The Sweet Ice Cream*

One day I was eating pizza. That's when I saw someone else eating an ice cream. I wanted to eat one too. I asked my father if I could have ice cream after my pizza.

"Yes, of course you can, David."

The next thing I knew, I was running to get an ice cream.

My mother told me, "Don't run, David!" That's when I fell down and hurt myself.

"David, what happened?" she asked.

I explained to her that I had tripped on the sidewalk. She just shrugged her shoulders. Even though I was running and fell, she still bought me an ice cream.

I was so happy eating my ice cream.

Before we returned home my dad and I had to buy a birthday present for my mother because soon it was going to be her birthday. Then we went to my house. That's when my father played with me.

That night my uncle, who lives in Miami Beach, Florida, came to my mother's party. So did all my cousins. My mother's birthday was great.

Then we planned to travel to Orlando, Florida, and my mother said it was for my birthday.

"Yes," my father said. "Yes, yes we are going at 5 pm tomorrow."

We got to the airport and we ate food first; then we got on the plane. I was super happy. Then we arrived at Orlando. "Can we go to Magic Kingdom?" I asked. And we did.

Then in Orlando, we found a cave. That's when my mother

asked, "Where are we going to eat?"

I said, "Yes, yes. Eat."

Then we ate at KFC. Five stars. Hah, hah, hah!

Then my father announced that we could go to Miami Beach. He told everyone that "David said we should go."

Of course I agreed, "Yes, yes, we can go."

When we got to the beach, my uncle was there. Because he was already in the sea, I jumped on top of him in the waves and found myself super happy to have him there. Then later, at his house I talked with him and we played games. That was so much fun.

Then we went onto Chicago, where we played in the snow. And it was so cool. I had the most fun day in my life. That's what I told everyone.

I also said, "My dad is good father and my mom is a good mother. I love them both very much."

# My Best Days in Lebanon

When I moved to Lebanon, I was thinking this is going to be a good time. I had four cats and one day I had to bury one of them. When we arrived in Beirut, the capital city of Lebanon, it was time for my sister's birthday and my cousin's birthday. We ate cake and ice cream. It was cool.

I didn't have any friends at first, but then I met a girl named Banat, who introduced me to her other friend, Nana. The three of us became friends instantly.

But I told them that we were missing two people, my sister and my cousin. We looked for them and found them. They liked them too and we all became friends. We played together every day. We didn't have school at that time so we played all day long and sometimes at night too. Three weeks passed and I was so happy.

One day I was using a spray for hairstyles and it got in my eyes, which became red. I was crying and it hurt so much that my mom put cold water on both eyes and they stopped hurting. Then we went to the hospital and they cleaned my eyes and I was okay. After I felt better we went to the store to buy toys. Then we went back to the hospital.

We asked our dad, "Why are we back at the hospital."

"Your mom is having the baby soon."

Dad was so excited; he was jumping side to side and soon my mom had the baby and the baby was named Larin and my dad said, "What a beautiful name for a baby."

That's when my mom told my dad, "No more kids. Four is enough."

My dad told my mom, "One more and we're going to Panama."

The second day I got to carry the baby. Her first word was my name. I had another sister, but she plays tricks on me. So, I loved my little sister more; she's very cute.

Soon enough it was time for school to start again. I was thinking, "What do I want to go to school for?"

My mom told met that I should be cool and go to school.

That's when I told her I was scared to go to school.

She told me, "You're going to be okay."

She also told me to tell the teacher if anyone hit me.

The next day, though I was still scared, I recalled what my mom told me. When it was recess time there was a girl who pushed me. I told the teacher and the teacher informed my mom.

That's when I took things into my own hands. The next day I pushed the girl back and I told her, "Girly, you are so mean!"

She told me, "Sorry!"

But I didn't believe her. She cried to me, "Please, please, please. Accept my apology."

I told her, "Oh! Okay, so you are really sorry?"

"I am," she answered, wiping her tears away from her eyes.

Amazingly, after that, we became best friends, playing together each and every school recess and sometimes after school too.

# The Ice Cream Store

On the ground floor was an ice cream store owned by one family. They had a dog, two boys, a mom and a dad.

The names of the boys were Sam and Carlos.

I remember how hot it was that day.

"That's why you came to the ice cream store?" asked Carlos.

Before I could answer, an officer, who had just entered the store, asked, "Are you all one family?"

I told him no, and then he asked, "Can I buy an ice cream?"

Sam's and Carlos' dad, who was at the counter, said, "Of course. What can I get you?"

Then on another day when we were all returning home from school, Sam asked his friend, Roberto, "Did you finish your homework?"

"No," said Roberto. "I will do my homework later."

Then a man in the street said, "Hello boys. What food do you like, fish?"

Sam spoke up and said, "You'll have to talk to my mom or my dad and they're working at the ice cream store right now."

The man knew about the store and had often bought ice cream there, so he went with his fish to try to sell them there.

An hour later we were all eating so much fish, me, Roberto, Sam and Carlos, their mom and dad, but not their dog because fish have bones in it.

Their mom was a great cook and had fried the fish for all of us to eat. Sam had invited us to stay for dinner and his mom said, "Okay."

All Roberto and I had to do was call our own moms about it.

For dessert, we all went down to the ice cream store and had whatever ice cream we wanted.

# The Dog

When I was little I had a dog named Amy. I loved to play with her, but one day she died. My mom called my dad and said, "Francisco, you have to come and take little Amy away."

I didn't know anything. When I was growing up many things happened to me. My life was bleak and I was very sad. That's why I am telling this story.

But a girl named Marta said "Wow! That was a crazy dream. Wow! Wow!"

So, my name is not Laura and I don't have a dog named Amy; its name is Moody and my dog is not dead; it is alive.

I don't have anything that's dead, while life is life and dreams are dreams.

There was a dog that looks familiar. That is strange. I went to sleep again, but again the same dream. Then I see the dog again and then I see a fox in my dream. Then I wake up again. Wow!

"Mom, I can't sleep or think about dogs. No, no, no, no, no!"

It's an invasion; a dog invasion.

Then another dream.

# The Best Family in the World

Once upon a time there was a girl named Sofia who had the best family in the world. It was morning and the mother said, "Good morning, it is time to eat."

Sofia said, "What? It is too early for the family to eat."

Dad said he would like to go to the pool!

Mom said, "Eat everything first, then we will go to the pool."

So, they ate everything and went to the pool.

Sofia went in the water. She said, "the water is very cold." Her father agreed.

They were all happy because they got a message that Sofia's uncle was coming, sometime around 11.

In preparation, Sofia put on a beautiful dress, along with a pair of purple shoes.

Dad said, "Sofia? You're uncle is here."

That's when Sofia ran downstairs and opened the door.

Her uncle said, "Hello Sofia. Would you like to eat a pizza?" She said "Yes."

The whole family went out to eat pizza and ice cream too.

When they got back home everyone was tired and the uncle told Sofia, "Pleasant dreams."

So Sofia dreamed. The next day she woke and walked around the house and saw the uncle, who smiled and said, "Good morning, Sofa."

Sofia said "Good morning, Uncle. Where are my parents?"

The uncle responded, "I thought you would like hot chocolate."

Sofia said, "Yes, hot chocolate." Then she saw her parents who entered the room.

"Good morning family," greeted Uncle. "I have a surprise. We will all go to the Hotel Sofia in Panama, which you will love."

The family was very happy. When we arrived at the hotel, there was a woman who said, "Hello, Welcome to Hotel Sofia. I will show you where your room is."

That next day the uncle, who had other plans, suggested the family go to the beach.

They said, "Yes, let's go to the beach."

There were a lot of people at the beach and then my father saw a sign that read, "Danger! Sharks! No Swimming!" It meant none of them could go in the water.

The mother said, "Well, we traveled a long way for this trip."

And Sofia's dad suggested, "We can go to another place." But they didn't find another place.

That night they were going to sleep in the family car. That's when father told them he had a friend who lived nearby. But he hadn't seen that friend in years.

When they arrived at the friend's house, Sofia exclaimed, "Wow! It is an enormous house." "Yes, it is," said Father, who pressed the doorbell.

A woman answered the door.

The father said, "I'd like to see Catalone Sandwich."

The woman invited them inside the house.

Catalone, who wasn't wearing shoes, greeted them. "Hello. Can I help you?"

The father asked if they could stay that night.

The man answered, "Yes, of course. You and your family can sleep in this room."

"Thank you," said mother.

The family slept through the next day.

When they were ready to leave, the father said thank you to his friend.

"Come any time," his friend replied.

Both were shaking hands at our car.

# *The Stolen Bag*

One day I was going to school, along with my mother and father. I didn't have to study, so I left my book bag in the car. My dad and mom were going to meet a friend in a restaurant. He left the car in a dangerous place and someone broke the window and stole my book bag. The next day a man from Venezuela called. "I found a big bag that says Vitoria Mitre." My mom and dad said, "Yes, yes, yes, yes!" We went to get the book bag. I was a little scared because maybe he could be the one who stole the book bag.

Thankfully he wasn't the one who stole the book bag.

Later, when we got home I went to sleep. Then the next day I went to school like everybody else. I told them that my book bag was stolen and that I got it back. It was incredible.It was a miracle. Not even I could believe it. Everyone was asking how it happened.

The teachers were like "OMG!" I told them it is true and it was a miracle. My book bag looked brand new. It was not dirty. It was really clean. It was even cleaner than when I got it.

The next day, at 8:30 pm, I went to the movies. I bought popcorn, a hot dog, and some soda. We were going to see *God's Not Dead*. I loved that movie. It was very nice; I liked it a lot.

When we arrived at the theater, my dad said, "Go to the bathroom before the movie starts." I told him I didn't need to go to the bathroom. When we got in, the movie had already started.

A short time later, I said, "Dad, I need to go to the bathroom."

Of course my dad was not happy with me because he told me to use the bathroom before.

"Vitoria, you have to wait now because I asked you earlier and you said, 'No.' Remember?"

Suddenly I didn't need to go, so I said "Okay Dad. I won't go."

While the movie was finishing I ran to the bathroom.

I learned a lesson that day that even when you don't need to to use the bathroom at least try to go.

The next day was Friday. It was the girls' turn to play football. I hurt my foot.

# *Gone to Guatemala*

One day I was preparing my backpack because we were going to Guatemala. The next day was Friday. I was so excited because my grandmother told me that we were going to stay in a hotel called Santo Domingo. My mother informed me that it was a museum and that it had statues, birds, and music.

The first day of travel we were flying on an airplane and when I we got to Guatemala, I remember stepping down from the airplane and a policeman drives us to the hotel. When we arrived we found out we'd be staying overnight in the rooms of a priest and a nun.

The next day we went to get our breakfast in the hotel's dining room with a buffet. My father was already getting his food. My mother said to me, "Come Alejandra, let's go see what we want to eat." We go into the dining room and it is the longest cafeteria I've ever seen. When we get there we already want to eat everything.

We ordered pancakes, eggs, milk, hot chocolate, coffee, juice, water, bacon, and more. I liked this hotel a lot.

After eating, I ran around the hotel. Then my mother told me that the hotel used to be sacred place for priests and nuns. I like how it feels now. When I entered the hotel is was hot and inside it was cool; there was beautiful music playing.

For dinner that night, we dined in the restaurant of the hotel. I ate chicken with potatoes and ketchup. I liked it a lot.

After a good night's sleep, the next day we go with some friends of my father to see the church and more of Guatemala. There was a kid named Javier at the church, which was very big with large stain glass windows that had drawings on them in many colors: red, black, blue, white, and orange.

When we were going back to the hotel, Javier said, "We never passed this way before" and my mother said, "Maybe we are lost?" But we weren't lost. We arrived back at the hotel and my father, mother, and I go to our rooms. We showered and dressed before sleeping.

The next morning we left the hotel to find breakfast. We go to a place to eat pancakes. My father said something, but I don't remember what. Later we met friends of my father.

Dad said, "Hello Howard." He was the father of the boy named Javier, who had a sister named Vivis. We all went to visit another church in Guatemala. We stayed out a long time.

# The Big Separation

Once upon a time there was a girl named Alexandra who went to Boston School but she just got bad grades and she didn't concentrate on her studies. The other kids laughed at her. She had problems with her parents. She cried all day. She thought her life was the worst life ever. She didn't have friends. But she had an aunt who took care of her when her parents were separated from her.

One day the aunt waited for Alexandra to come home from school. The aunt told her that her teacher had called and told her that Alexandra's grades were very bad. After being confronted by her aunt, Alexandra went to her room and cried for several hours.

The next day she made two new friends, but the girls were super bad. They told her that in order to be cool, she had to get even worse grades than she was already getting.

She didn't tell her aunt what she was planning on doing because she knew her aunt would not approve.

Meanwhile, Alexandra had been searching for her grandfather and finally found him. His name was Publio. After spending only two weeks with him, she declared Publio "the best grandfather in the world." She had the best moments with him. She even forgot about the two super bad girls.

But days passed and one day she saw them. That was while she was waiting for her grandfather after school. Her grandfather listened in on their conversation in which the girls were planning something bad. That's when Alexandra's grandfather told her that he didn't like her friends and that he was going to pick her up from school every day. She was angry at him because of this, but she still loved him and she found ways to meet the bad girls at lunch or during recess at school.

Years passed and her grandfather died. That's when she finally stopped talking with the bad friends and looked for new friends who didn't try to get her in trouble and really cared about her. That's when her life got better and her grades went up and she was happier than ever.

# The Mystery of the Cake

Once there was a cake store and the owner was named Millie.

She was the only worker in the store. Then she had one visitor at her store. It was her friend, Audry.

"Hello, Audrey," Millie said. "I was waiting for you to help me make some more sugar berry cakes. Those are the special of the day."

"Okay, let's make some more," Millie said.

"But I can't," answered Audrey. "I need to go to my singing class."

"But you don't like singing."said Millie.

"I'm sorry," said Audrey. "I need to go."

So Audrey went away and then Millie baked all the cakes, then she went home.

Meanwhile Audry was planning to rob the sugar berry cakes at the cake store.

"Oh yeah, revenge is so sweet, like those sugar berry cakes," said Audry to herself. "What Millie did to me hurt a lot."

Millie and Audry had once been bffs (best friends forever), but one day Audry saw Millie with another girl having so much fun.

So now Audry's plan was to steal the cakes, and learn about the secret potion of the sugar berry cakes that were so delicious, without Millie ever knowing anything about it.

# In Canada With a Problem

One day I was with my family at the mall shopping. It was in Toronto, Canada. We were going to buy ice cream, candy, chocolate, brownies and all the sweet things in the world.

We went to eat at a place that was called Popeye's. We were visiting our cousins in Canada.

After two hours, I was on the escalators (electric steps) and by accident I put my foot in and it got cut and there was a lot of blood. I was wearing flip flops at the time. When we went to buy shoes the girl saw my foot and she cleaned it. And she put a cream on it and told me to "put the cream on your foot every day until it is better."

But I couldn't sleep. I told my mother, "Mom I can't sleep, please help me. I need your help."

My mom told me, "You can sleep; it is your imagination keeping you up."

So that night while eating candy, I started jumping on the bed. My brother entered my room and I smiled at him.

He told me "Aliyah stop jumping on the bed and stop eating candy."

I told him my feet were hurting and that I couldn't sleep. I also suggested we find something entertaining. Then I looked at the clock; it was midnight.

We woke all our four cousins. We popped a bag of popcorn and ate it while watching Netflix in the TV room. Before long, our grandmother came out of her bedroom. We ran and hid after turning off the TV; she was in the kitchen to get water and she went to her room again. We came out of hiding and started jumping on the sofa. I should have been happy, but I felt like crying.

Then my mom and dad came out of their bedroom, running.

They told me "You are our little princess, but you are going to be punished."

I said that it wasn't fair and then they chose a "punishment that keeps you in your room without a computer."

My dad told me, "You can't talk to us like that. You need to be respectful."

My mother said, "Okay Aliyah, then your punishment will be not going to the movies tonight."

I told my mom, "Please let me go to the movies tonight. You can change my punishment to no computer for one week."

She answered, "Okay, Aliyah, but don't do this again."

I was scared. My mom screamed a little bit at me and was mad at me because I didn't obey the rules but she was right.

I went to the movies that night, and a photographer approached me and asked, "Where is Aliyah Patel; where is she?" I told the photographer, "I am her!"

She said, "What happened to your foot?"

I told her, "It's not your problem and why do you want to know?"

She told me because "We are going to put you on the internet."

That's when I yelled, "Jeez!" All the people in the room could hear me.

Then after one week I was so popular.

It was crazy, but fun.

# *The Airplane*

One sunny Thursday I was with my family. We were going on a trip to Panama City. My brothers and I were scared, but then our father told us: "Don't be scared, children."

This was when we were boarding the plane.

Later there was some turbulence that started on the airplane. And I was very scared. I couldn't even sleep. That was when my mom said, "Please don't be scared, honey. It's just a plane. You need to sleep more otherwise you'll be tired."

A little time later we put our seat belts back on. That's when we were eating and there came big turbulence and my plate of food fell. But it didn't matter to me; it wasn't that good anyway. Then one of the flight attendants came and started to clean me and my seat.

In English I said, "Thank you, miss." She didn't understand anything I said, but then I realized that she only spoke Spanish! All day I was speaking in English and they spoke Spanish. This is probably what will happen at the end of the world! No one will speak the same language! Anyway, I got bored and started playing with my mother's cellphone.

Some time later we landed and all people started clapping. I asked, "What are they doing Mom?"

My mom told me "They're doing what people did back in the old days when an airplane landed."

I said, "Okay. Now I understand."

While we were waiting for one of my father's friends to arrive at the airport after work, I shouted, "Why is it so hot here?"

I was dying! In Spain it was not so hot. It's really cool. My brothers were also dying but they were checking their cellphones and one of my brothers was talking on his phone, or so I thought. But he was really in a virtual girlfriend game and then I started laughing. "Ha, ha, ha."

Then my brother said, "Why are you laughing?"

"Because your with a virtual girlfriend," I told him.

"How did you know?" he asked.

I said, "I saw it the last time just before you covered your phone."

My brother complained to our mom and then she screamed at me: "Don't do it again, do you hear me?"

"Yes, Mom," I said.

Then one flight attendant said to my mother, "Shhh, please! There are babies sleeping."

My mom was really angry but she looked away from the flight attendant and at her cellphone; that was the thing Mom did when she got stressed.

When my dad's friend finally came, he said to me, "Hi Beauty."

Then we got in his car. While he drove and talked, I saw many of the things that are in Panama that are not like Spain

One day, when I started to miss my friends in Spain, one of my brothers said to me, "I care about you! Okay sister?"

"Okay," I responded. Then gave him a big hug.

# *The Antics of Wilmer and Humberto*

Once upon a time in Chacao, Venezuela, there were two best friends. One of them was Wilmer and the other was Humberto.

One day, they were invited to a girl's party; so there were mostly girls at this party except for Humberto, Wilmer, and one other boy named Gabriel, who also wanted to play with us.

Later on that day, Humberto said "How about if we do something?" And Wilmer answered "Like what?" Gabriel also became interested. Altogether, they came up with a plan to fill a bucket with soda and use it to spill on the girls.

They quietly crept into the living room where there were no adults and hung the bucket with a rope. Once the girls entered the living room, SPLASH! They all screamed "AAAAHHHH!"

Of course, all the girls were sticky and soaking wet! They wanted to get the boys back somehow, and a girl named Alejandra said "Don't worry, I have a plan."

"What do you plan on doing?" Valeria, the birthday girl, asked.

"We are going to use our Nerf guns, that's what!" said Alejandra smartly.

To be continued!

# The Scary Mountain

One day I was on a trip with my family. We were going to ski. I saw the mountain and I said, "Mom and Dad, I am scared."

They told me, "Don't be scared, Son."

When I finally got to ski it was more scary than fun, even though I had a special backpack.

On the way up the mountain, while we sat in the chairlift, my parents were warning me not to fall and have an accident. That's when we let go of the string connecting us to the chairlift. My parents shouted to my brother who was just ahead of us, "Fast, grab him!"

But he couldn't reach me, and I started skiing down the beginner's trail on the mountain, and it was very cool. I didn't fall!

Then I met up with Francisco at the bottom of the mountain, and he was eating something sour that made his face look funny.

Then we went out to eat, and ate a lot. Then we drove home. When we arrived there I went to sleep. I dreamed that I was skiing and I was the best!

*Home on Another Planet (Grade 4)*
## Foreword by Teacher Joe Haviland

Part of our 4th grade curriculum in science this year at Boston School International (BSI) was on the planets in our solar system. I wanted us to do more than just orbit the planets by reading about them in our *Fusion* textbook.

You remember them? The inner, rock and metal planets of Mercury, Venus, Earth, Mars, and the outer gas giants Jupiter and Saturn, along with Uranus and Neptune, the ice giants. And let's not forget the dwarf planets, including the reassigned Pluto or MakeMake, which sounds like a sushi dish!

I wanted my students to do some hands on work with the planets in our universe, while learning about their individual characteristics. So I suggested that we build that same solar system in our classroom. My eighteen students got messy with balloons, strips of newspaper, flour, water,and washable paint, excitedly creating a paper mache universe within the four walls of our own classroom space. Outside our door, we put up a sign with big cutout letters, "Welcome to Our Space!"

Inside the classroom, we still maintained our bulletin board, throughout the 2nd trimester, that proclaimed a line from the movie version of Roald Dahl's *Charlie and the Chocolate Factory* in which Johnny Depp's Willy Wonka says, "Good Morning Starshine. The Earth says, 'Hello!'"

Our classroom has been a creative, buzz-light year, space throughout this year in whatever subject we've studied, in whatever language, English, Spanish, and even Mandarin.

In this chapter of *More of Less*, I thought we'd carry on some cross curricular capers. (I love alliteration and hope I've taught my kids to love it too this year.) So, we blasted off from our science studies on space into writing imaginative stories about each of us living on a different planet or moon than Earth. As for me, I'd have chosen Mars to live on. It has water as ice and if Matt Damon could grow vegetables, I'm sure I, an avid gardener, could too. Maybe even coffee?!

So, come explore the universe (non-fiction and fiction) with my 4th graders in this next chapter. It's packed with fun and lots of originality with each prescient pupil zooming out into the universe and reporting about what he/she experiences. (Don't be surprised if some of them end up on the same planet together, now and then; that's what friends do!)

# *The Day I Go to Venus*

*Facts About My Home Planet,*
*VENUS*
Venus is often called the Earth's sister planet.
NASA's Mariner 2 made a successful flyby of Venus on
December 14, 1962.
Next to the Sun and moon, it's the brightest object in sky.
Named after the Roman goddess of beauty and love.

Venus is the hottest of the planets in our solar system; this is why I picked it to live on. I'm used to hot weather living in Panama.

A day on Venus is longer than a year. Can you imagine that? It takes 243 Earth days for Venus to rotate on its axis. Venus orbits around the sun in 225 Earth Days, compared to Earth's 365.

Both are similar in size to each other, with only a 638 km different in diameter. Venus has 81.5% of Earth's mass.

One of the reasons I chose this place was because of these things that are the same.

They both have a central core, molten mantle and a crust.

What's my story? I was on a mission to go to Venus. So I traveled to that planet and when I got there I found out that it wasn't at all like Earth. That's when I went running back to the Earth. But then I changed my mind. I stopped back at Earth long enough to refuel and pick up my family. We took everything with us. I thought I was crazy when my Mom told me, "We are going to live on Venus."

We would have a new air conditioned house on Venus where I'd live with my mother, father, brothers, and sister. We flew back in my rocket ship.

I wasn't too happy about leaving Earth a second time. And of course it was too hot on Venus, averaging 864 °F.

Ten years after I tell my mom, "Oh, Mommy, it is time for me to live on Earth again. I am leaving this crazy planet."

"Wait a minute. Are you really going?"

I told my mom, "Yes. Why not?"

So, then I asked my brother Mohammad, "Do you want to come with me?"

"Did you ask Mom?" he said.

I told him I did and then I said, "Let's go. I will marry on Earth," I said.

"Okay, that's wonderful," my brother said.

"One moment," said my brother Issa. "Are you going to Earth?"

"Yes of course."

"But I want to go, but I don't want to take you with us."

"Why?" I asked, a little hurt by what my brother said.

"Because you're crazy! Ha, ha, ha."

That's when I said goodbye.

Three months later we are on Earth again. I am so happy.

And one year later I am already married. I ask my brother, Mohammad, "Do you know what my husband's name is?" Before he can answer, I tell him his name is Abdallah and he is a famous Arabic artist. "We just had a little girl. Her name is Dania and she is a very good artist like me. I remember when I was famous? She will be famous too."

"Baraa, did you know that Mom is coming today?" asked Mohammad.

"Seriously?" I asked.

"Yes, she's coming, and so is Dad and our brothers and sister."

I know now that we can continue with our entire family back on Earth.

That's all of my story.

# Moon Exploring

*Facts About My Home, Jupiter's Moon*
*Europa*
It is the largest of 63 moons of Jupiter.
I have a subterranean salt-water ocean, proved by NASA.
The only moon with its own magnetic field.
Larger than Mercury and Pluto; could be classified a planet
if it was orbiting the Sun and not Jupiter!

I'm planning to go to Jupiter's moon. Europa, because I heard it is a cool moon and also a very cold place (You can find temperatures as low as -171 degrees Fahrenheit). Based on the fact that I love winter season, I decided to invite my family to an excursion to this lovely planet.

There's my sister, Sheyla, and my mother and father. They were all very excited to go to Jupiter's moon with me.

The day before we left, we barely could sleep and we were all wondering what we will find out there in space during our trip.

Finally the departure day! We woke up early enough and went to the spaceport. We took the first shuttle to Europa Moon.

During the trip we were able to see all the galaxy and after a few hours we got there. It was hard for me to find out that all I read about this moon is true. The first thing we found out was that there is a frozen ocean and the fifty layers of clothing that we were wearing was not enough to keep ourselves warm.

We decided to stay in a French-style hotel that was all covered by a thick layer of ice. The ocean view rooms we stayed at were really awesome. The hotel was beautiful, quiet, and very comfortable.

To our surprise, we found the moon was dying; that's when we decided that we were going to save the moon.

Our family decided we should clean up all the contaminants in the area to help to clean the air needed for the many plants, animals and people that live there to breath.

During the four weeks we spent there, we recruited, and convinced most of the families we met there, and started a local movement, oriented to make this beautiful place the greatest place I have ever explored with my family: Europa.

On our way back home, we were wondering where we are going next. To explore and help to keep this wonderful outside world existing and surviving over the upcoming years.

Exploring Jupiter's moon, Europa, was just the start of knowing the unknown outside world.

# My Life on Jupiter

*Facts About My Home Planet,*
*JUPITER*
A day on Jupiter is equal to 9.8 Earth hours.
It's a planet with rings.
On Jupiter your weight would be 2.36 times your Earth
weight!
The large red spot on Jupiter has been created by a
storm that has lasted over 300 years.

One day I was watching TV and then the TV said that in one week our planet Earth was going to be hit by a comet. That's when I was running around like crazy, warning people that the world was going to be destroyed.

Then I told all of the boys in my class that I would take them to Jupiter.

I was playing a video game I really like, and I heard a knocking on the door ; it was Mark.

"What the heck are you doing here?" I said.

Mark answered with a question, "What's Up?"

Then I let him enter.

Just as I was ready to play the video game, now with Mark, there was another knock on my door, and it was Aristides.

I asked him, "What are you doing out of your house?"

He didn't have an answer. He just said, "I want to stay here."

So all three of us played video games and made plans to blast off with our friends and families to Jupiter the next day, before the comet hit Earth.

# Playing Cards on Uranus

*Facts About My Home Planet,*
*URANUS*
Spins lying on its side, like a barrel due to a previous collision.
Orbital speed of Uranus is 14,763 miles per hour.
Named after the Greek god of the sky.
Has some nights that last over 40 years!

Uranus is one of the cold planets. It's cold, okay. The coldest planet in our solar system. Maybe as cold as -216 Celsius. LOL! I'm watching TV here on this planet I've moved to.

After that commercial break let's continue.

I had to do more things. I played cards. Then I welcomed my family who had come for a visit. We all wore helmets and special suits when we weren't inside.

My PS3i played my favorite video games all day, while my family visited. They even brought my cat and his little house. I was happy they'd be visiting for a couple weeks before heading back to Panama.

"I guess you won't need air conditioning anymore," my mom said, "But you'll have to continually stay warm here on Uranus."

After helping them to get unpacked, I called Juan Jose and said, "Yo, whats up?" He was living on Jupiter now. We had a long conversation on Skype.

One of the things I'll miss here is wearing a costume for Halloween. I'm not sure how I'll celebrate any of the holidays here on Uranus. I want to buy blades, for ice skating.

I want to go back home, maybe for Christmas, and have a big family reunion. I'll take my rocket. I got an astronaut's license a couple years ago, when I was still living on Earth.

When I got home Juan Carlos contacted me, and we got together and I told him all about Uranus, and he told me about Pluto. We promised to visit each other at our new home planets.

# Copycats on Eris

*Facts About My Home Planet,*
*ERIS*
Astronomer Mike Brown discovered Eris.
A Dwarf planet, part of the Kuiper Belt.
An icy object orbiting beyond Neptune.
Takes 560 years to orbit the Sun.

Teacher Joe said, "Aris, you should go to Eris because it's like your name!"

So, I imagined that I went to Eris and then I said, "Hey, I hate this planet. It's way too cold." That's when I returned to planet Earth.

Then I heard Amy and Patrick fighting for the moon and calling each other "Copycats."

Teacher Joe continued with his story, saying that "Aris returned to Earth after visiting Eris and ended up living in Los Angeles, CA, next to a world famous dancer who happened to be one of my classmates from fourth grade at Boston School."

At this point, I continued imagining my story, in the future of course.

That's when Jose Humberto shouted across the classroom. "I moved there too! I told everyone, 'Hey, this is my planet now!'"

That's when I yelled, "Copycat!" to Jose Humberto, of course.

He said, "Aristides, we both deserve to live on that planet." And I responded, "Sure, you can live with me. Okay?"

He agreed and said that we could be "best friends forever."

In my imagination, I watched Rubio's spaceship land on Eris.

Rubio said, "Hello Aris."

I said, "Hello Rubio. How have you been?"

Six hours later, when Rubio finished with his minions, I said, "I don't see Jose Humberto."

All Rubio could tell me was, "I finished with the minions."

Then Jose Humberto showed up a few minutes later. That's when I gave Rubio a ride in my rocket to Saturn. Jose Humberto wanted to join us, and we said, "Okay."

When we landed on Saturn, Rubio and Jose Humberto wanted to play soccer.

I was getting ready to return to Eris, a week later, and my mom called on Skype. She says, "Aris, why don't you ever visit me?" She was still living in Panama.

That's when Rubio and Jose Humberto had a great idea, "Let's all go visit Earth together. You can see your parents and we can see ours!" This time we went in Jose Humberto's new super fast rocket.

# My Life on Mars

*Facts About My Home Planet,*
*MARS*

Many massive volcanoes on this planet.
The atmosphere made up mostly of carbon dioxide.
It is known as the Red Planet because
of the dust clouds of iron oxide.
The temperature of this planet varies from 32 °F to -148 °F.

The National Aeronautics and Space Administration (NASA) picked only five people to live on Mars and I was one of them. We were chosen for our creativity, knowledge, and abilities.

My team and I went to Mars on a spacecraft named ZAR 5. The mission to Mars cost around 20 million dollars. We were going to connect with a satellite called *Translator* that takes astronauts wherever they want to go.

Being on Mars is not boring because we are always building interesting and new things. I can always order Papa John's pizza from the moon and also on my birthday my dad sent me a PS4 and, if you can believe it, a tennis court.

I can wear anything I want on Mars, but the only thing is that I always need to put on a special chip that creates oxygen all around me.

Today my friends visited me on Mars. Not all of them of course, but some of them did.

They were part of a mission that NASA assigned them in

the farthest galaxy we know. Sadly, my friends do not have what I have on Mars. In other words, they don't have a smart chip and a house like mine.

In their galaxy, they don't have enough water and food for all of them, so they were basically trying to find a way to survive. The only thing that my friends still had was their own spacecraft, and they were running out of time. That is why we suggested they use a worm hole to get from their galaxy to ours, so in that way we could help them. In other words, our suggestion was their best option for them to go home and save their lives.

My friends couldn't finish the mission that NASA assigned them because a black hole was swallowing the whole galaxy. The galaxy was called Curvegiantworm, and it's called that because of its great worm shape and because it has the biggest worm hole of the known galaxies.

If you don't know what a worm hole is, let me teach you. A worm hole is like a piece of paper that you fold in two parts and you make a hole in between the paper, so anything that is smaller than the hole can pass easily through it. That is why you can pass a lot of galaxies in a short period of time because of the magnitude of the hole.

So, in other words, the universe in the paper; the holes are the worm holes, and anything that is smaller like the ship can pass through the worm hole easily.

When my friends arrived on Mars they were almost dead. That is why we needed to feed them and also we gave each of them a big bath because they were in really bad condition. That's how they recover so fast while they were staying with us on Mars.

But it's not what you're thinking! Just to be clear we put them on a machine that gave them a bath and then the same machine gave them some new clothes. Otherwise, it will be kind of disrespectful or weird if I was the one to give them the showers. After all they are my friends, and I will never do that to Patrick. I wonder what he'll say, maybe, "What's wrong with you?!" I'm sure that he would say something that's going to be very funny.

There were only three people on the mission to Curvegiantworm galaxy and they are Patrick, Daniel, and Gabriel, my friends. They all just wanted to go to their peaceful homes.

So, getting back to the bath stuff, anyone I know who is my age does not let others of their same age shower them! Who'll do that? Maybe someone who is crazy.

Well, my friends were really hurt and in bad conditions and maybe without us or without my help they wouldn't be back right now. Maybe technology was our big ally because if we didn't have this advance technology they'll be in heaven right now.

When I was checking my satellite, that warns me about any problem that is approximating to our planet, Mars, I realized that the black hole that destroyed the galaxy Curvegiantworm also swallowed other planets such as Saturn and it was on its way to swallowing Jupiter. We were lucky that the sun of Curvegiantworm wasn't swallowed by the black hole so that means a new galaxy can be created in billions of years.

My team, which is my family and me, have big doubts about how the black hole came to the Milky Way galaxy and we just keep thinking to try to find an answer and Daniel has a pathological fear of the black hole and Patrick has an aversion to a black hole.

Daniel said, "God isn't enough!"

"Maybe he just wants us to be happy," I said,

"Why are we here?" Gabriel said, almost in tears.

"To visit us and no one who is at my house should feel unsafe," I said.

"I know I must have hope. But do you?" asked Patrick. "Do you?" he repeated.

Dad said, "Stop! You are just making it worse. If we hadn't have told you that you had to use the worm hole to come here and have more days to live, you'd all be dead right now. So, if I was you, I'd be thankful."

"Zulmy, are you thinking the same as me?" I asked.

"Yes, AJ. Are you thinking about it or not?" Zulmy said.

"Can it be?" AJ said.

"What are you thinking about?" Mom asked.

"How the black hole entered the worm hole of Curvegiant-worm and maybe it wasn't a black hole. Maybe it was created on purpose," I said.

"We have to get to the worm hole right now!" Daniel shouted.

"Let's collect as much food, dirt, and metal as possible," AJ said.

Suddenly everyone in the house was in the kitchen and they were so focused on figuring out how to send a message to every government on Earth and every industry that studies space. There were only five people that could make decisions on Earth; so it will be easier to find a solution.

The kitchen on the inside was all blue. It was opposite Mars. My house was also technological and intelligent that if you asked it something, the house will answer you. So, we decided to eat something at 11:30 am because we wanted to use the whole afternoon for thinking and researching about what was going on in the black hole and if it was real or not.

When we were about to start lunchtime, none of my friends knew how lunchtime on Mars was done, so we had to teach them how. The desk that we used for lunchtime was a technological table where everyone could order any type of food that they wanted and it would all be free!

Well, I ordered some nuggets with barbecue sauce and fries with some ketchup. My family and friends ordered Papa John's pizza and I ate a slice of their pizza because I was really hungry. So, in other words, I ate my lunch and part of theirs.

During the whole lunchtime nobody talked at all; the only thing I heard when we had lunch was the prayer we said before lunch and the crunching sounds made by people who were eating, especially Patrick , because he woke up at 11:20 am and he was starving because he hadn't eaten breakfast that morning.

Later on, after we finished eating, we realized that Mars and Earth were like magnets because big forces can control them.

Just when we knew how to move Mars and Earth, the black hole was swallowing Mars. So when I was trying to look at Mars' sky, I looked at Earth's sky instead. The big question was, "How can we observe the Earth if we are supposed to be on Mars? Well, the black hole turns into a big *Translator* so it somehow brought us to Earth.

How? That is a big mystery.

Why? It's not every person who deserves to go to a place will get to that place. And if they don't it is because the universe has a magnificent plan for them and they just don't know about it.

Special Thanks to: God, Zulmy Carolina Escobar, Teacher Haviland, my parents, and brother for inspiring me – RAE

# The Life on Pluto

*Facts About My Home Planet,*
*PLUTO*
In 2006, Pluto was no longer one of the
Solar System's nine planets, and newly labeled the largest
"dwarf planet".
Temperature ranges from -235 °C to -210 °C.
Pluto is 18% the size of Earth .
Atmosphere of nitrogen, carbon monoxide, and methane.


My family decided to move to Pluto; it is not like Earth, which is special because we have a cat on Earth, but we're talking about Pluto

On Pluto it is boring and it is so cold (-390 °F). But not the Coca Cola; it's just right! The food is hot. We came here by rocket ship, blasting off from Earth and arriving three years later. That is unfair! I came here with Hector, who's still a kid like me. Young, young, so very young; funny too.

I was at Boston School before I traveled to Pluto. Personally I recommend that school to you. It is the best school I know. Here on Pluto I cannot play soccer! There are no official sports teams here.

I am packing my back pack and I am going back to Earth for good.

In one hour from now we'll be lifting off to Earth, but I'd rather be exploring Mars. On Pluto I am exploring. I find out that people here are always drinking Coke.

I'm back in class here at Boston School; Jose Humberto is reading a story; it's funny. It's 1 pm. Soon it'll be time to go home where I'll get my rocket ready for my next space trip later this summer when school is out. Not sure if Hector will join me; hope he will. It's better to have friends join you in space.

# My Life on Saturn

*Facts About My Home Planet,*
*SATURN*
Flat at its poles.
Sixth Planet from the Sun.
Rings of Saturn are made of water ice.
The day of the week, Saturday is named after Saturn!

I came to Saturn in a special rocket that exploded its way through space. After we arrived I spent a lot of time sleeping but I did get a chance to see the rings at night. I like to drink water that we brought with us as it's natural.

I called my mom and told her to come here because this planet is very pretty. So my whole family is here now and that makes me very happy.

I cook for my family here on Saturn. They like my cooking.

In our 10 room house the doors open with your hand. You put your hand on the door and it scans it and opens automatically.

I've opened up a dance academy here on Saturn and have invited Camila and Veronica to come and visit.

The other day I told my family we should plan a trip back to Earth. My family said it was a good idea. I need to go to Earth; my family too. We travel in one special rocket and I see that Earth is still okay. My family and I land in time and they thank me so much. I tell my family they're welcome, and how much I love them all.

My family and I returning to Earth is very good because I needed Earth; I missed it a lot. Saturn is good but Earth is better for my family.

———

# My Solar System Life

*Facts About My Home Planet,*
*NEPTUNE*
Almost four times the size of Earth.
Has worst weather in our solar system.
The windiest planet, with up to 1,240 miles per hour.
Absorption of red light by methane causes blue color of
planet.

I traveled to the coldest planet, Neptune. My friends, the two Ricardos (Rubio and Escobar) went with me. We took turns driving the plane to Neptune. Rubio, Escobar, and I played soccer on the way to Neptune.

I told them, "Neptune is cold, so I think we all have to bring a coat."

But Rubio said, "No, we don't have to bring a coat; we just have to play. Ha, ha, ha!"

Escobar added, "I have to check the computer. It's not working!"

"Oh, we don't have WiFi!" I tell him and that's why he can't get internet.

After a long trip, we landed on Neptune. I was happy to make contact with this special planet finally. But my body was freezing, icy cold. I looked at the two Ricardos. They were shivering with ice on their bodies too.

That's when I said, "I told you we should have bought coats."

That's when a hungry monster was looking at me.

"What are you doing here?" the monster asked all three of us.

We were all afraid that the monster would eat us. But at that moment, he said, "Don't worry. I won't eat you. Ha,ha,ha!"

"Oh my God," Rubio said. "This is just ploopy."

At this time the Solar System Police (SSP) were on their way and promised to catch the monster and help us get our rocket safely back to Earth.

The other day Rubio, Escobar, I, and our friend, Patrick, set out for Venus.

That's when Rubio said, "Now we have to take a lot of coats when traveling to Venus."

"Yes, we have to take more coats," Patrick agreed, "and we have to call one extra person."

That extra person was Juan Jose. When he arrived, he was singing the solar system song we learned in Teacher Joseph's class. "We are the planets of the solar system," Juan Jose sang. He went through the whole song, and then said, "Hello guys. How can I help you?"

"Yes, you can, but that's the only reason you can come to Venus with us," I said.

Suddenly I said, "Rubio, let's play football." That meant soccer to us since we grew up in Panama before we started traveling the universe.

"Okay, but I'm Barcelona," Rubio said,

"Okay I'm FC Bayern München" I told him.

Juan Jose added, "I want to play too. I'm Red Madrid."

But Patrick and Ricardo were playing. There wasn't room for one more player.

We're now in Venus. It is too hot! There was one bird flying but it was hot that the bird died soon after I saw it. We went back to Earth and wrote this story for all our readers.

I am now 49 years old and we are going to the moon. What?!

The Two Ricardos said, "Yes, we are going to the moon to play soccer."

But we didn't really go to the moon for a very long time. When we finally thought about a trip to the moon, I said, "But now you are very old, like me, 73."

"So you don't want to go? Okay, so we can stay," Patrick suggested. "But the Earth has gone broke."

"What the heck?" I asked.

Patrick was acting like one crazy rabbit, running all around. He said, "Oh my goodness."

"So what are we waiting for? Let's go," I said.

We were back in the solar system, headed to the moon, when Patrick said, "What about my house, my girlfriend, and my car back on Earth?"

I reminded him, "But earth is broke, your girlfriend broke up with you, and your house and car are both broke too."

Then Jose Humberto showed up. We were on the moon at that point. We don't know how he got there! "Wow!" I said. I'm jumping high without gravity; we have one practice soccer game with Rubio. We are all on one team and the other team is made up of all stars, Messi, Neymar, Suarez, and Di Maria. Am I dreaming?

"Oh that's strange!" Patrick said just before the game started.

The football game started. Messi's team first. Messi passed to DiMaria and then to Rubio for the goal.

# My Life on Eris

*Facts About My Home Planet,*
*ERIS*
Named after Greek goddess of strife.
Previously called Xena.
So far from the Sun, the atmosphere sometimes freezes.
Comparable to surface of Pluto, it is rocky.

I was traveling on the fastest rocket in the world, faster than the speed of light. It was called a Mayancat. I was heading to Eris where it was so cold. I had a friend of mine invent a special item. He was called Ricky Rubio. No that's not true. Ricky Rubio is a Spanish basketball player, who played in the NBA with the Minnesota Timberwolves from 2009 to 2015. The real inventor was my friend, Ricardo Rubio.

Now living on Eris, that special item keeps me hot unless the electricity goes off. I know it's charged by something else beside sunlight. If we relied on solar power there'd be a big problem. You see, the sun doesn't shine here.

I had company and he was Aristides, a friend of mine and he had minions. The only thing is the minions don't speak Spanish but they understand.

We started building a house; that's when we saw the spaceship of Ricardo Rubio.

Then we saw the minions and we told the minions to build our house, so it was fast. We got inside and the invention Rubio made was working without a battery. Okay, we need to make a special bubble and Rubio interrupted me saying, "We can take pictures of my rocket."

I went, "Alright!" But there was someone strange here, and I was trying to get my gun out when I said, "Put your hands up."

Everybody was affected. It was only my teacher Joseph. He was scared and he ran. I told Aristides and Ricardo Rubio, "I am the captain!" I was the only one with a gun, so they agreed.

# *Saturn*

*Facts About My Home Planet,*
*SATURN*
Almost 1,600 Saturns could fit into the Sun.
Saturn rotates so fast that it bulges at its equator.
Many astronomers consider Saturn the most beautiful
planet in the solar system because of its rings.
Storms here can last for months or years.

Okay, so I got here on a purple, heart-shaped, metallic rocket. So what? BTW (by the way) NOT on one of its thousands of moons. DUH! Like HELLO!

It's super fun because it's made of helium and hydrogen. It's like walking on clouds. So to you who are reading this, "You should TOTALLY come."

Being here alone except for Veronica had been TFTBT! (Too Fun to Be True) Get used to it; I use initials! So, beat it.

It's super safe here on Saturn. We asked President Obama for an okay and unlike Teacher Joe he let us in without sending us away first to give his okay. Veronica already has a family. She married a famous dancer called Manuel.

Right now Veronica is bugging me to leave. We need to start planting potatoes. Hi again! I'm on the Hab: it's a fancy way to say, "special room". There's a gas storm outside. Veronica is telling me to start securing the Hab. But I think she can handle it. Since there's nothing to do (BTW I mean fun) when the storm is over... Wait what the heck was that? Whoa! Veronica is IMPALED! I should have helped her! I'm taking out the antenna stuck in her arm. Yucky! Voila! Done. She's coming alive! Yay, call me Supergirl!

Newsflash: the Hab is blown away! Fortunately I got my EVA, from NASA, space suit on. So does Veronica! I'm on the space ship, ready to leave this DANGEROUS place! Wait, my cell phone! Getting off. There, grabbed it! Running back, Veronica almost left me! Going back to Earth. A SP (safe place). When we get home we are going to zero gravity (a fun place) to get french fries and water, plus have some fun. After that we're getting some ICE CREAM. Yummy!

Great, no, Veronica and I are stuck in Jupiter's pulling-force and we can't go on. "My food!" Veronica was eating and B3 opened Letting All The Food Out! Thank U! I told Vero.

"What have u done?"

And she told me, "GO OFF!"

I told her, "No way!"

She pushed me off and I (with my EVA suit) united with the extra spaceship and recruited Amy, picked up Vero, and the girl I met, on Earth at NASA, and we came back.

BTW, I picked Amy up on the moon. We came back 2 Saturn 2 pick up stuff and Steph (short for Stephanie), the girl I met, told me, "I wish we could go to other planets, like a tour!"

I told her, "Let's ask NASA!"

That's when Vero said, "Count me in."

And so we ended up packing.

Now we're just seeing how the spaceship we are on gets lost in another galaxy. Good that I picked Vero up. So, we got in the spaceship and we are leaving Saturn. The trip is one month long to Earth.

1 MONTH LATER... We are landing on Earth ready to go to zero gravity! And eat ICE CREAM! And of course have another SLEEPOVER and super cool experience.

# *My Life on Jupiter*

*Facts About My Home Planet,*
*JUPITER*
Named after the king of gods.
Largest planet, mass of Jupiter 318 times Earth's mass.
Takes 10 hours to complete a full rotation on its axis.
Clouds on this planet are made up of Ammonia Crystals.

I am on Jupiter. It's a big black and orange rock. Jupiter is much bigger that I had imagined it would be. Jose Humberto and I play soccer every day. Then I see a person I think is Juan Jose. And we all play cards with Jose Humberto like we used to do back on Earth.

Juan Jose and Jose Humberto ask, "What can we eat?" and I say that there is black meat. Juan Jose says thanks and we all eat a delicious meal with my friends. We play soccer. Juan Jose and I win. I say to Juan Jose, "There's a storm, we have to go to the rocket; we have to run."

Jose Humberto asks, "Where is the rocket?"

Juan Jose and I answer, "We don't know."

So we go and see if we can find it and eat chocolate. That's when I ask, "What do you want to eat?"

Jose Humberto says, "Cereal and milk"

While eating, I tell Juan Jose that Jupiter is the biggest planet in our solar system.

The next day, the storm continues for a long, long time.

We finally find the rocket and we blast off to the other side of Jupiter where we'll build our house.

# *My Life on Venus*

### *Facts About My Home Planet,*
### *VENUS*

Surface is very dry; used to have water but dried up.
Planet is 68 million miles away from the Sun.
Interior is with iron core and molten rocky mantle, just like
Earth's.
It takes 243 days to rotate on its axis.

My name is Sebastian. My family and I decided to move to another planet. We grew tired of Earth. We wanted to go to the planet, Venus. Okay, now we're on Venus and this is my life on Venus. One day on Venus can be super hot. I was the only kid, next to my little brother, on Venus. Of course, we had our dog, my mom, and my dad too. You don't know how much I missed Earth.

Oh! My mom is ready to eat.

"Mom, what are we going to eat?"

"A rock that we found, Sebastian." she answered. "Do you want it?"

"Okay," I answered, not really wanting it.

"No, we're not really going to eat a rock, honey. I was just joking. We actually have some frozen sushi I'll be defrosting. Do you want some?"

"Obviously, Mom!"

When we finished eating, a big storm came and we quickly entered the ship my father had built. And we raced back to

Earth. All my family, including me, said at the same time: "Ah!"

Back on Earth, I told my friends, like Jose Humberto and Juan Carlos, that I missed them, a lot! Obviously!

I ran through my house and we all ate some ice cream. I was happy to be back with all my friends We had a pizza party that was super cool.

Thank you for reading this.

# *Neptune*

*Facts About My Home Planet,*
*NEPTUNE*
It has eight moons, the biggest, Triton.
Average temperature is – 200 °C .
Triton orbits in the opposite direction Neptune orbits.
In 2003 NASA proposed to send a spacecraft to Neptune;
it was scheduled for 2016 and never happened.


I finally got to Neptune by a super rocket. It took three years for the super rocket to get here. It was faster than the eight to twelve years predicted in a proposal by NASA. On my journey I ate the same thing every day: rice.

It's fun living on Neptune. It's cold and you can play with ice and snow. I'm alone because no one is bothering me. I also get to play football, by myself.

Sometimes I wear a monster suit just like you wear clothing, and I can control his arms and legs. It's not cold inside the behemoth (another name for monster that I learned in spelling in 4th grade) suit because the monster suit is very warm. You can do whatever you want in that thing.

Before they joined me, I asked my dad, "Do you know that on Neptune it is -200 degrees Celsius?"

"No," answered my dad, who my Teacher Joe once said, "Your dad looks a little like actor, George Clooney."

Then not so long ago, I said, "Hello Family. Welcome to Neptune." It took them four years to travel through space to

Neptune by another super rocket.

My family said, "Hello Nicolas. We brought you a new house to sleep in."

"Thank you," I answered.

The next day Jose Humberto came by and told me, "Iker Casillas is here!!"

"No way!" I responded.

"Who is Iker Casillas?" asked my father.

For some reason, we didn't tell him who Iker Casillas was (FYI: he's a Spanish footballer, who plays for the Portuguese club, Porto, and Spain's national team, as a goalkeeper). I don't know why. All I remember is that we had a big pizza party.

Then after two years of playing non-stop football with all of the 4th grade class, which was no longer in 4th grade by that time, we came to Neptune from Earth and said: "What happened?" Juan Pablo said, "I'm going to go to Uranus!"

Then the rest of the class, including Teacher Joe, who was still teaching 4th graders, traveled to another planet, just like Juan Pablo had done.

# *MakeMake*

*Facts About My Home Planet,*
*MAKEMAKE*
Discovered March 31, 2005 before I was born!
Second brightest Kuiper Belt object.
Name comes from the creator of humanity.
Mostly is without a gas envelope.

I am a boy who is nine years old. I am going to MakeMake. How am I going? I am piloting a specially designed rocket ship of course! I was watching TV in Panama and the TV reporter said people should consider leaving the Earth because it's stupid.

So, I packed up and was on my way through space to in the Super Duper to MakeMake.

MakeMake is a dwarf planet that's very far from the sun and also very cold.

Okay, at the moment I don't know what to say. But I plan on writing a book about my adventure.

Some day I'll return on a special spaghetti ship to Earth and go to the TV station.

For now, I'll enjoy my trip to MakeMake. So, for now this is my story's end.

Credits go to Hector, Hector, and Hector!

# My Life on Saturn

*Facts About My Home Planet,*
*SATURN*

Galileo, first astronomer to discover Saturn's rings, but he
thought they were satellites instead.
Diameter is 74,500 miles.
Saturn's distance to Sun is 938 million miles.
Saturn's rings are the only ones that can be seen from Earth.


One time I lived on planet Earth, in Panama with my parents Gustavo and Carolin, and my dog, Lucas. My parents and I wanted to explore other planets. So, we built a special space ship to go to another planet, Saturn. We boarded our spaceship, all four of us, and blasted off into space.

When we got to Saturn it was kind of cool. We lived there for a year. In that year we had everything we needed, including food and water.

I must admit it was a little boring as I didn't have anyone to talk to that was my own age and there was no TV.

Regarding my clothes, I wore an astronaut suit that was both cold and hot.

After a year, I wanted to go back to Earth. I started to think about Panama and how warm it was there and how I had the rest of my family and friends there. I told my parents that I wanted to go back to Earth. They understood.

What I remembered most about Panama, besides it being so warm, was all the friends I still had there.

As I said, it was a little boring on Saturn and I felt homesick. I felt a little better when I played with Lucas.

When we got back to Earth I realized a lot had changed.

I wondered where Ricardo was. I heard he had become a mechanic, but was he rich or poor? I also wondered what happened to Delfi. People said that she would marry Matthew. I wondered if it was true, so I searched for Matteo and Delfi. I thought that Vana would marry Matteo. I knew that Luna had married boyfriend, Simon.

I found Delfi with Matteo, Ambar with Sebastian, and Luna with Simon. Amanda was there too, but by herself.

Amanda said, "Mia we haven't seen you since the graduation. Your project in Saturn worked perfectly."

I said, "Yes, it did and it's true I haven't seen you since the graduation. I am 24 now and you are 25?"

"That's right. Well,I want to invite you to my wedding."

"With Mark?" I asked. Everyone at the table looked at me in shock.

Amanda said, "With Luis! Yes the wedding is in three weeks."

I couldn't believe it as Amanda and Luis were nemeses back when we were in school.

I eventually found Matthew. He was a mechanic. I went where he worked and visited for a while.

"Mia I haven't seen you since the graduation," he said like everyone else. "You know about Amanda's wedding?"

"Yes," I answered.

"I wonder if you would like to go to the wedding as a friend?"

I said, "Yes, of course."

Three weeks passed and it was time for Amanda's wedding to Luis.

Luis kissed Amanda when the priest said, "You may kiss the bride." Then there was a big celebration after the wedding ceremony.

# My Life on Saturn

*Facts About My Home Planet,*
*SATURN*
Pioneer 11 did first flyby of Saturn in 1979.
Diameter is 74,500 miles.
A year on Saturn is equal to 29.5 Earth years.
Saturn was named after the god of agriculture.

Can you imagine living on another planet? I can because I"ll tell you all about our trip to Saturn. That's super right! Okay, let's stop wasting time and start the story. First of all, you want to know about how I got there, right? I rocketed to Saturn in a super duper jet-packed shoe with glitter. Of course I didn't go alone. I'm traveling with members of my family and Camila's too.

When we first got there, we saw Saturn's super-duper rings. Did you know that Saturn's rings are thousands of moons? I did. I loved Saturn the first time I saw it up close. Of course, living on a different planet than Earth, I had to decide what to wear. That's when I picked a super cute space suit where I press a button and it automatically changes clothes.

Then I got ready and went to explore and found Camila and her family and her twins. Then I said, "Hello, Camila. How are you?"

I invited her and her family to eat dinner because it was dinner time. We ate a delicious meal. Of course I cooked.

"What a great meal," Camila said.

We ate some meat with vegetables and rice. Then later we went outside and saw Earth because you can see Earth from Saturn We also went to ride bikes because Saturn is the flattest planet but it was hard because Saturn is made mostly out of hydrogen.

After eating, we rode bikes. We went to see the 150 moons of Saturn and also the moonlets. Camila and I went to see the rings too, leaving our spouses and kids at home.

The next day was awesome and in the afternoon we saw a girl and the three of us, Camila, the girl, and me screamed "Ahhh."

We stopped to ask her "What's your name?"

She said, "My name is Stephanie."

"Nice to meet you," said Camila

"What are your names?" she asked.

"My name is Veronica."

"My name is Camila. When did you get here?"

"I have been here three years."

Camila and I stared at her with our eyes wide open!

"Three years?" we both said at the same time. "We have been here only two days!" I said. Then I invited her to my house.

On the road the three of us became close. Camila and she became even closer, and I have to admit I got a little jealous. When we got there, they were laughing and they looked like they were having so much fun. Then I interrupted and said, "Do you want something?"

"No thank you. I don't want anything," responded Stephanie. "I love your house. It's so big and so nice!"

"Thank you," I responded. When she turned around to look at Camila, I stuck my tongue out. She didn't even have the least idea that I did that.

Later on that day, Camila said, "I'm going to go around the planet. Do you want to come?

"No thank you. I need to make dinner for the kids," I said, prevaricating.

So Camila and Stephanie went away and I started thinking three seconds later that I can call Amy. So, I call her and when she answers, she's like, "What do you want?"

"I need help with a problem," I said.

"You need me to solve your problem?"

"Yes. I thought it was obvious."

"So, you call me to solve a problem between you and Camila without Camila?" she continued.

"Yes. Thank you for understanding, Amy"

"Okay, Veronica, tell me your problem and I'll try to solve it."

"Well, we met a new girl, and Camila got too close to her and I got a little jealous."

"You saw a new person?"

"Yes, but concentrate on my problem. I'm not cooking you dinner for nothing,"I said.

"Okay, I'll come but better cook me dinner," she said.

"Ok, I'll cook you dinner, but come quickly because my kids are not being so impeccable."

"Okay, but my rocket will need some fuel."

"Deal! Just come over as soon as you can."

"Okay, coming."

She said she'd be here 20 minutes later. She got here and told me "Where's Camila?"

"Walking," I said.

"Okay, maybe you thought about it another way than it is?"

"Maybe, but I don't think so."

Then Camila and Stephanie arrived.

"Hi Amy? What are you doing here?"

# My Friends on the Moon

*Facts About My Home, the*
*MOON*
Has no atmosphere or wind; footprints will stay there
for millions of years.
Diameter is 2,160 miles.
Fifth largest satellite in our solar system.
Neil Armstrong was first person to ever walk on the Moon.

Do you know how much fun I'm having on the Moon?

When it was morning I asked my mom if I could get the heck out of Earth and go live on the moon with Rubio and Mark.

She said okay. I couldn't believe it. Maybe she was carefully concentrating on creating for her class (that's alliteration), a test in Mandarin and didn't realize what I had just asked her.

So, all three of us packed up and used one of the fastest rocket ships of all. My friends and I blasted off.

We were all investigating the moon. When we finished investigating, we took a rest, eating cheese pizza and drinking soda. We kept eating and drinking.

We were having a crazy party. We were playing with light sabers and fighting each other. I was like OMG! All of us were building rockets to shoot them off and explode them.

Then I saw a rocket from the Avengers and they were attacking us. I used a rocket launcher. I shot at them and they went KABOOM! (That's onomatopoeia for those of you who don't know. I learned about it from Teacher Joseph in writing/grammar class). That's when Deadpool showed up in his black and red suit. I couldn't believe it! Deadpool! "What are you doing here?"

That's when Rubio, Mark, and I got to my ship and we blasted off to Eris, leaving Deadpool behind on the Moon.

When we landed on Eris, I spotted the camp first. It was so cold but when I got to the camp I saw Jose Humberto and Aris, who both kept on sleeping. That's when we started monkeying around and that's when JH woke up, and he was happy to see us. Aris kept on sleeping, as did my brother Dennis. Hey, how did my brother get to Eris? He later confessed that he stowed away on my rocket ship and got to the camp before us and found an empty bed there, so he just went to sleep.

I was waking up Aristides and he said, "You and Amy were calling each other Copycats." That's when I told him how we knew, it was because he kept it in his diary.

I was building a big house with five rooms. We all entered the house (all of us); then JJ came. He knocked on the door and I said, "Who is it?" Then I opened the door and he said, "SHUT UP!"

So, I said, "It's time to dance."

JJ started dancing first. But Mark asked me to play a video game he liked a lot, and Rubio soon joined us.

JJ took a picture while we were playing. Then when I finished playing, I destroyed the house with a wrecking ball.

I went to the rocket ship with my friends, but not with my older brother, and after saying goodbye to Jose Humberto and Aris, we blasted back to Earth because I didn't want to stay on Eris forever.

Back on Earth, we started celebrating and playing PS4, a game called fifa16. We were playing turn by turn. That's when

I saw a note from Sebastian, but there was nothing on it. He entered the house like a spider. I was like "OMG, did you teleport?"

He said, "No! I was sneaking on the top of the roof, okay?"

I took a break from playing the popular video game. That's when I slept and dreamed about what Aris and Jose Humberto were doing.

*In the Future Sci-Fi (Grade 5)*
**Foreword by Teacher Katie Lamb**

---

In fifth grade we like to inquire into lots of things, as we practice becoming better students and better citizens. Some of this inquiry leads us to wondering what the world will be like in the future and how decisions made now might affect life then.

With these questions in mind, the fifth grade class, of Boston School International, took off on various adventures to the future where each student faced different issues; many of which were caused in our current time and escalated as time went on.

In writing these stories they hope to make people more aware of current problems, so that their future and the future of those to come can be a clean, safe, and happy one.

# The Time Machine

My name is Ramon and this is the year 4440. Around me I see the buildings are destroyed, the streets are dirty and filled with blood, and the sky is black. The only people with me are Maria and Diego. We can't find anybody else. This is not my home. I am from the year 2016. A lot has happened in a short amount of time. I am going to tell you how I got here and what happened.

One day I was at home with my dad, my father is a scientist and he wanted to build a time machine. His lab was in the basement of our house. The lab was illuminated with blue lights because it helped him to concentrate better. The walls were white and there were a lot of computers and machines and cables all over the floor. My father didn't like for me to go into the lab because he said it is dangerous.

One day I got curious, and went to the lab when my father was asleep. That turned out to be the worst decision I ever made. I entered the lab and I looked around me. I didn't notice the cables on the floor. I was looking at data on the computer when I tripped on a cable, pressed a button, and fell to the floor. The button activated the time machine and in seconds it sucked me in.

When I woke up of course I wasn't in my father's house. Instead, I was in the street and everything was broken and destroyed. This is definitely not the city where I was born. The first thing in my mind was to fix the time machine. I suddenly heard someone yelling for help. I ran towards the sound.

"Help! Help!" I hear again and again.

This is when I met Maria and Diego. The zombies wanted to kill them. I took a rock and I threw them at the zombies. The zombies were distracted and Maria and Diego escaped.

All three of us sprinted away from the zombies, who were chasing us. I tripped on a rock and Maria and Diego kept running. One zombie bit me as I was standing up. I screamed, "Ouch!" That's when Maria hit the zombie with a pipe, and it let me go. She and Diego hurriedly helped me up and we continued our desperate fleeing, We got to a safe place and Maria patched me up.

It turns out that Maria, Diego, and their siblings had been running away from zombies for many days. They told me that the entire world was now destroyed. They had been looking for other people. I told them I am from 2016 and I want to go back home. They don't believe me. They thought I was crazy.

Maria, Diego, and I had been traveling together now for many weeks, but sadly we had not found any more living people. I also started to get sick. I was cold all the time, my head hurt, and my eyes felt very dry. I was always on the lookout for my father's time machine. Maria and Diego did not think I would find it.

I was alone in the abandoned house that we were using to hide from the blood-thirsty zombies. Maria and Diego were out looking around. I opted not to go with them as I felt so under the weather. At one point I was dreaming about their return where they would tell me that they had found the time machine.

Then I woke up and continue to feel sickly. Soon I fell back to sleep.

When I woke up again, Maria and Diego were back. Maria gave me some medicine they found in a hospital where there were no medical people. Almost immediately after I took the pills I felt better, but then I felt worse again. That's when they told me, "It might not be possible for you to go back to 2016."

I decided that I would stay there and survive if I had to, but I would never give up hope. Maria and Diego were now my good friends. I don't think they will ever believe me when I tell them I'm from the past. They think it's just some cockamamie story that I imagined.

But we have each other, and that's what counts most. We are helping each other; we will make it. Soon, I'll be almost well again, not so sick anymore; but I will learn to live with a persistent cough that will never go away.

# *Traveling to the Future*

My science project went wrong and I end up in the future.

My name is Issa, I was with my friend when he said, "I am better at playing basketball then you." I told him, "No, you're not!," so he tried to hit me. I ran away from him and ended up at the science fair. That's when I fell down on my project, which tragically transported me to the future.

Now, I ask, "Where am I?"

A boy named Santiago, whom I just met, tells me, "We are in 3068!"

"3068?" I ask and it's obvious I'm shocked.

"Yes, 3068. And there are robots here that are programmed to eliminate humans. We are in great risk."

Of course back in 2016 my friend was still looking for me. But I was somewhere else where he could not get to me.

Santiago and I travel to a factory, but when we get to the factory I see that it is dark except for robots with bright red eyes. When Santiago and I see this we make a run to the portal. But he doesn't want to risk entering it. I say goodbye to him at the portal's entrance, thanking him for his help. Then I dive into the portal, and am transported back to the present again.

That's when I meet up with my school friend and he says, "Where have you been? I was concerned when I couldn't find you."

"It's a long story," I tell him, "I was in the future."

Now it's my 2016 friend who doesn't believe my story about time travel. Just like Santiago in 3068 didn't believe me either!

"Issa, can you go back to the future again?"

When I tell him that yes, I probably can, he's jumping up and down, so excited about going to the future with me. He's forgotten all about our basketball match.

"Okay, let´s go to the future," my school friend says.He's fearless! Back in the future, we find Santiago, who asks, "Why are you here again?"

After I introduce my friend to him, I tell him, "We are here take you to the present."

He now finally believes me that time travel is possible, and has overcome his own fear of it. So, all three of us get to the portal but it turns out that only one person at a time can go to the present, 2016. We decide Santiago must go to our present.

After Santiago enters the portal, we go in search of a science fair here in the future. Sadly we can't find a project that can help us to get back to the present. We might end up staying here in the future forever.

"What are we going to do in the future?" my basketball buddy asks.

But then we go back to the portal, hoping that something will have changed.

I yell, "Oh look! I can't believe it. The portal is open."

My friend thinks "Santiago did this from the present. He must have! Lucky for us."

This time we're both able to enter the portal and when we arrive back at 2016, there's Santiago. So, we are going to be okay in the present.

"Thank you, Santiago," I say.Now we are at home.

# Brink of an Unknown World

Apollo 20. The only one of its kind to ever attempt interstellar travel. On the brink of an unknown world, floating towards the endless-black of the wormhole.

"Engines Check!" Captain hollered. Fire immediately sprang from the back of the rocket and it propelled us forward with great power and speed. Moving tremendously fast the rocket broke the speed of light; it was incredible and a joyous occasion for everyone on board. No one had ever done this before but great things also come with repercussions.

The corridors started shaking, the fins started trembling, and the whole ship started falling to pieces. Captain threw himself to the floor. His legs were torn from the recent movements and his shirt was ripped by fragments of glass.

Blood was coursing down his chest and he was in unbelievable pain. Suddenly an explosion came from nowhere and there were flames everywhere covering the entire ship. Captain didn't know what he was going to do and his mind was working hard, but just when he stopped concentrating, a piece of debris hit him in the back of the neck and he was out cold.

Later that day, NASA was saying farewell to five valiant astronauts, thinking that they were all dead.

A deadly noise echoed through Captain's head. "Where am I?" muttered Captain. A barren wasteland stood before him. Mountains of sand towered everywhere and there was no living organism to be seen. Everything was calm, but in the distance Captain could see a storm brewing and it was going to hit very soon. He felt like dying just there, but his survival instincts made him keep going.

Trudging through the sand for ages and no sign of anything, Captain's legs were aching and his bruises from earlier were throbbing, but he came upon a shelter of some sort and stumbled into the door. He fell through and found himself starring at a man.

"Hey! I thought I was the last one left?" The man spat.

"The last what?" replied Captain, feeling very uneasy and confused.

"The last human of course! What else?"

"What?!"

"Just like Einstein said, 'I don't know what World War 3 will be fought with but World War 4 will be fought with sticks and stones.'"

"What?"

Suddenly, at that moment the ground began to tremble and Captain instinctively sprinted for the door and away from the house, believing he'd be safer outside. Then, in mere seconds, the house, where the man had just been making a reference to some guy named Einstein, was blown up. Captain could hear his screams echo around the now violent sands. Captain knew what had just hit. The Storm.

Captain meanwhile was not completely safe; he battled to shield himself from the deadly sand. There was nothing he could do really, but he persisted nonetheless, keeping as low to the ground as possible. Rocks started to grow from the surface of this planet and lava started shooting from all the crevices of the earth. It was clear now in Captains head that he was in the future and that it was mankind that had turned Earth into this calamity.

He stayed alive as long as he could, eventually succumbing to death. Captain stumbled forward, fell and watched the world burn. His final words were: "We are traitors to God, please Lord, forgive us."

His eyes shut slowly and he was the last human to ever see the light of day again.

# The Polluted World

(Hassan: An expression used to refer to some one who is immensely cool, and has style unrivaled by anyone else.)

I just came back from the future. 4,949. I want to tell you about my incredible story.

Now let's begin. I am now here in Whoopi Land on April 30, 2016 in the late afternoon; it's a Saturday. I am walking in the street and it's scary because it's filled with human-eating Carnival people and headless zombies. I'm with my Russian girlfriend, Anastasiya, from the future, who tells me, "Honey, you're the best kisser ever and I'm going to miss you when you make that dangerous, deadly mission to the future."

"How do you know about that?" I asked, thinking about how I had already been to the future and didn't want to return.

"Because Mr. Clinton (that's what Anastasiya calls me even though she knows my first name), I am your girlfriend from the future."

"What the heck!" I shouted back at her. "But you never told me about that before!She told me, "I didn't tell you, honey, because I was scared that you were going to be, you know сердиться (sil-dit-sa), angry."

"Okay, but who are you now, in the present?"

"The same person that you know in the future. Anyway, let's talk about the mission." Anastasiya said it's about the pollution you think you already cleaned up. "That's all I can tell you right now. That's all I know."

So, I said goodbye to her in the way we did it in the past,

or was it the future? We shared a three fingered left hand salute like they do in the *Hunger Games*, where they kiss their hand first and raise it in the air with the three middle fingers up and the pinkie and thumb down. Then we whistled that sad mockingbird (a cross between a jabberjay and a mockingbird) *Hunger Games* whistle. You know the one? "Toot, toot, toot, toot" that means that someone was going to die.

I run to my house and I put my future jacket on and got inside the time machine. As I make preparations for my second time jump into the future, back to the year 4,949, I recall my first trip there and I want to tell you about it.

The future is cool! When I arrived there I saw big houses that could fly, along with flying cars. In the future they don't have Ebola. That means nobody will die because of Ebola.

It was rainy when I got there. I realized that it had only taken me a minute to get to the future because the time machine was faster than the travel of light.

They didn't have dollars in this future place called Astonia, which sounded very Russian to me. They had a gold coin with a diamond in it. As I said, everyone, even the poor people, live in flying houses with a lot of televisions inside, even in the bathrooms and the kitchens. Their culture was monotheistic. They only ate bananas. They have a lot of electricity from solar power. You have to go to the future, where I saw worms inside the mud.

But sadly, there was a lot of pollution here. I was walking in the street. Everybody was dying because of the air pollution. After that I went to swim in the river and I saw the pollution. When I was in the river I saw dead fishes. Then when I got out of the river I went to the forest. In the forest there was a lot of dead animals because of the pollution. I couldn't see it was so thick. Animals were almost extinct. Then a lot of people started to help clean up the pollution.

So many people were cleaning. When I was in the street cleaning trash one man came to help me clean. When we were finished I did a commercial about cleaning up pollution. Nobody listened to me, at least not at first. Only my friend and a person named Leo came to clean up the pollution. After that we went to the river. Everybody had a big basket in their hands.

In the future, we cleaned the Rio Gatun. After that everybody started cleaning and cleaning and after 27 years the world had no more pollution.

# *The Future!*

One day, I went to Central Park, in New York City. with my dog Scott. My name is Alvaro and I am from the 21st century. While at the park, I saw a black hole above me in the sky. The black hole started sucking up everything and everyone. That's when I started running away as fast as I could; my dog running faster. But then I tripped over a rock and fell, jerking Scott back with me. The black hole succeeded at sucking me and Scott inside. That's when my dog said something to me. I stood up and exclaimed, "I am in the future, wahoo!"

As of this writing, It's the 51st century, September, 5021.

The future? Wow! It's a blast. The people of the future love American football, soccer X7, and the hover board. Everything here is SMART. The cars and buses fly themselves. There are many types of houses, like flying mansions, underground apartments, and houses located in space.

I asked a young boy how many planets there are in this solar system and he told me that there are fifty-three planets and 3 suns.

The strangest planet is called Mamalocalia and has a temperature of -500° below zero.I also asked about the Statue of Liberty and he told me that there isn't a city called New York anymore. Everything in this strange world is controlled and run by smart and intelligent technology. Their cellular phones are implanted in their arm and they are able to play virtual games with them.

Oh, technology is amazing!! I am walking on the street with Scott, and some men are dancing hip hop to strange music, wearing gold necklaces; one astounds me with a smile of greeting.

I asked an intelligent person if people smoked each day and the person answered that one billion people smoked each day. I told him I was in shock. Again I noticed that the rivers were contaminated with black water. There were many trees on fire. Factories let loose black air causing the sky to be black. A lot of animals were hunted. They almost hunted my dog.

"Is that the biggest mountain?" I asked one person.

He said, "Yes, it's Everest."

I also found out about a gentleman named Pedro Fernandez, who died four centuries ago and I realized that was my uncle.

It was amazing because the continent of Asia was ice. Oceania was a wilderness. Antarctica was water where many species of animals became extinct.

I asked another gentleman about diseases and he told me there were thousands and some rare syndromes, which I found interesting.

While I was walking my dog, I met another person named Y and his friends. They all had dogs with computerized chips that when the dogs barked, they spoke in as many as 10 languages.

"Can you tell me where the robots are?" I asked them.

They told me that they were located in the street factories, which were all very dangerous.

We returned to talking about dogs in the future.

"My dog has 12 names and personalities," said Y. "The smartest is Pepito, the dullest is Louie, Pedro has allergies, Pedrito is the oldest, the youngest is Carlitos, Loambi and Alvarito are good at sports, the better looking ones are Josesito and Jaimito, the prettiest is Cristiansito, and the happiest is

Eddisito, who has a girlfriend named Nalicita."

As Y continued to talk about his multiple-personality dog, I was glad I had just one dog Scott with one personality and one name. It would get confusing otherwise.

Y told me that his dog or dogs were running very fast and ran over Cristiansito and Eddisito. That was terrible and then humans hunted Loambi, Josesito, Carlitos, and Jaimito.

"I lost my sweet Alvarito, but was able to catch Pepito the smartest one, and there were two puppies. It was so sweet when Eddisto kissed his girlfriend."

After we talked some more, we took a walk to the factory where Y and his friends put water in the robots, then disconnected their cables and the power. In this way they caused the destruction of this factory and others were doing the same throughout the world. One by one they were all destroyed.

# *My Trip to the Future*

Hi! Wow I just came from the craziest trip ever! I am 10 years old and my friends call me Cookie, but my real name is Natalia.

We are in the summer of 2016 during a tennis tournament and suddenly I was hit by a tennis ball. Boom! It hit me so hard that I was literally knocked out. A few hours later I opened my eyes and I did not know where I was.

Everything was so different. I saw flying cars and people talking to themselves. I was asking for help, but I felt like I was invisible to everybody. I decided to take a walk to figure out where I was and to my surprise I saw a billboard that showed the date: April 3045. OMG! This must be a nightmare.

"WHERE ARE MY FAMILY AND FRIENDS NOW?" I screamed to no one. Well, as the time passed by, I was starving and I went to a restaurant and ordered a pizza and milkshake. Money was useless and food was served in capsules. Can you imagine that? There are no green parks, no trees to climb, no bikes to ride, and worst of all no friends to talk to.

I started crying because I missed my family. Suddenly I fell asleep. A few minutes later I smelled homemade cookies. That's when I realized it was all a dream.

Now I am in my cozy bed next to my mom with a plate of real cookies and a glass of milk. Thank God it was just a dream.

# *Back to the Future*

One day there was a boy named Eddie who was building a time machine. When Eddie finished his time machine it was the year 2016 and Eddie was eleven years old. Eddie had a goal to go into the future. He wanted to reach 2019. He wanted to go in to the future in order to help the pollution problem.

Many years after he created his time machine, he accidentally pressed a button that took him to 2024. In that year, people have portable houses. Their phones and electronics have holograms that pop up at a push of a button. The reason why people have portable houses is because they believe that they should constantly be moving. Staying two nights in one place is not acceptable to them. These portable houses have portable back yards which come in handy because in 2024 people grow their food in their backyards. Everything they grow they use in the meals they prepare.

Eddie has observed how people in 2024 live and he believes that he can make a change in order to make this world a better place for them.

In 2024, while wandering the land, he noticed how much pollution there was all over. He was hoping that he could really help with this problem. The pollution was killing plants, animals, and ruining our world.

Eddie thought he could change all of this but first he thought that he needed to call his brother, David. He told him to come ASAP! Eddie told him to bring their recycle mobile. They were able to pick up half the trash that they needed to in order to start healing this world.

They went around in the recycle mobile looking for areas that needed the most help. They found many areas in desperate need of recycling. By just investing a little time and effort doing what they loved doing, they could make a difference in this world. They reached their goals by making that difference and were able to help mankind make the Earth a better place.

# *The Future*

I'm in the laboratory of my white-haired, 80-year-old grandpa. Everywhere I look there are all his old books. It's snowing outside and I'm helping him build a future transporter machine. That's when something sparkles in the machine and then a blue circle-shape portal appears and a sudden wind comes from the portal and drags us towards it and we can't help but enter. Then suddenly, "Bam!" I faint.

"Wake up sweetie, wake up," Grandpa calls. I wake up and sit up to see what is wrong.

I find out that we are now in the future, It is the year 3010. There are helping robots that fly into space, flying cars that pop and sparkle. People live in houses with thousands of floors. The weather is hot and it is snowing because a kid went to Alaska and brought snow clouds back with him.

Everybody has to wear jackets and shorts. Also you can go skiing and camping but at your own risk. When I was taking a walk I saw the robots teaching in an invisible school. I also saw this billboard it read, *Mt. Everest this way. Be careful with what you find!* Because of this people believe it's not safe going outside anywhere, especially into the forest where Mt. Everest is. They think that the trees will go zoom and capture them, put them to sleep, and eventually eat them. In 3010 people keep talking about how dangerous Mt. Everest is. Also they say that during three weeks of the year, three persons will climb Mt. Everest and find it completely missing.

Suddenly I hear a noise, "Arianna, sweetie."

It is my grandpa calling me from his laboratory, which is

now in the future.

"What's wrong grandpa?" I ask.

"Take a look at this news," he says, holding a newspaper up in front of me.

I read the newspaper article about Mt. Everest. It said, "The last three passengers to be seen climbing Mt. Everest were Hailey, Michael, and Sarah Liendo. They haven't been found since."

"Oh look they have the same last name!" I say.

"Exactly, honey," My grandfather goes on to say, "That means they are your sons."

I am so surprised and I know right away I need to search for them on Mt. Everest. "Grandpa I have a solution. We have to go to Mt. Everest and find my sons."

"Okay, let's go." he agrees. "But first we have to pack up water, lots of clothes, and grab a tent to sleep in."

We started to pack up as fast as a cheetah runs. Just in case we need to use it, I pack an ax(Kids do not use an ax without adult supervision). Then we head to the mountain. That's when I hear a loud noise: "RRAAAH!"

"What was that, grandpa?"

"I don't know but we'll have to find out."

I am so nervous my face trembles with sweat. Then it is night time, we set up our tent, climb in, close it and go to sleep. But then I see a shadow, it is like a monkey, and his hands are opening the tent.

That's when I quickly grab our ax and cut his hand off. As soon as possible he runs away. Then I close the tent and go back to sleep. When I wake up the sun is shining and I wake up my grandfather, who didn't know anything about the monkey last night.

We pack up and then climb up and up the mountain,

taking rest and water breaks now and then. Suddenly we find a cave. We travel inside it, deeper, deeper, and deeper until my grandpa and I are hit by something and we both faint. I wake up first, then my grandfather, we are both tied up with rope that's iced over. We look around us and see all these people in ice cubes.

Then I see a beast who says, "Welcome, to the ice monster cave, do you like our collection? Oh sorry, let me introduce myself. I am one of the ice monsters of the mountain."

I couldn't believe that there were people frozen in ice cubes.

But quickly I was able to untie myself and my grandpa, I grab the ax and try to break the ice, but it it's impossible. The ice monster laughs, "That ax won't break our ice power. It is too strong for you, human girl."

Maybe for the ice, but it works against all the ice monsters, who I quickly kill. Sadly, the ice won't melt and it is too strong for my grandpa's ax.

As grandpa and I escape the cave, I say, "At least now no one will ever be frozen again."

Inside, I feel miserable for not being able chop my sons of of their ice cubes or unfreeze them.

We head back to the village to tell the people there about what horror we saw.

# *The Big Adventure of Poroto*

I am Poroto the dog, who went to the future to save the world from itself. But then I am also Poroto, a dog, lost in the street in the year 100,000. A vedimial saved me and a kid adopted me. I was happy after that, for a while, until everything changed. The Black Hand was furious because I took a funny, fuzzy, fushia ball from a funny, fat, fuzzy cat. That's when I was sent to the year 100,000,000. The Black Hand said, "I AM SO ANGRY!"

When I went to the future, the five cities had changed a lot. There was a lot of trash in those cities and all the people were gone. There wasn't anything alive. That's when I saw that there were robots instead of live humans. There was no school, and we were constantly traveling in a spaceship, circling the Earth.

The ozone layer had a big hole in it and through that hole space trash entered the planet. It caused many toxic gases and trash on our planet. That's why people were now on a spaceship. Earth was no longer habitable because of all the pollution. We wanted to try and clean it up, but we needed to find other humans to help us and teach them not to litter. Though there are no humans living on Earth to trash the planet now, there is the Black Hand who's throwing more and more trash.

Fortunately I fought the Black Hand and won.

# The Technology War

My name is Pablo; I'm living in 2016, but I found out that I can time travel to 2123 faster than a rocket. When I traveled to space in my rocket, something happened: I accidentally pressed a button that turned my rocket into a time machine, landing me in 2123. For a moment I thought I would die because of the extreme speed, or I would have to stay safely locked away in the time machine when I got there.

In 2123 I learned how the world had changed.

It was an artificial atmosphere and robots were capturing humans like beasts. I didn't have much hope of living in this time, but then I met another human when I ventured outside my rocket/time machine, He gave me a weapon and told me, "If you see any robots shoot them." Then he told me that all the trouble began when humans started to believe only in technology, creating artificial knowledge, artificial human organs, and robots.

Yes, the world was full of technology. And full of robots. The robots were really mean. The human I met said they were all controlled by M.C.

"Who is M.C.?" I asked. They told me over and over that "M.C. is the Master Computer."

This M.C. wanted to create a technology world and make people believe in the technology god. M.C. created electronic brains and could control everyone's thoughts.

Soon it was time to fight against the robots. Of course no one had any idea on how to do that. I decided to start training myself. Nine months later I was ready. I got to M.C.'s castle. A bunch of robots where standing in front of the castle. I had to fight against them and finally destroyed them.

I entered the castle and shot at M.C. several times. He exploded and the explosion was so big that it sent me back to 2016.

# *The Apocalypse*

I just got back from the future and it was horrible.

My dad made me go to the future but I did not want to go so he trapped me in a timemachine and the machine kept doing this weird sound, "Pip-plop pip-plop, pip-plop." The year I time traveled to made me wish I was still in 2016. I think it was 4029. I am Sofia Riera. Now let me tell you about the future.

The future was bad; it's very bad

It's very black! You can't see a thing. There's trash everywhere. It smelled so bad that the odor can kill people, many of who live in the woods looking for food.

Here in the future, people get killed a lot because something in the future kills them. There are only a few people left in the world and they are trying to survive an airborne virus.

The apocalypse was really bad.

There were walkers and zombies everywhere and it was very bad. If they bit us then we would turn into one of them dead heads. We were trying to keep ourselves alive. I had to stop this, but how? And how will I save the world?

Then from the past, my dad contacted me. I don't know how. He told me he fixed the time machine, so I could go back and I did.

Now back in the present, I now know how it all happened and I can fix things so the future will be better.

# *The Time Hero*

I am Christian Vandervelde. Did you know that in the future Nutella and soccer balls can talk?

One day I was walking back home and a sausage bit me. Entering my house, I still couldn't believe that that had just happened, I always thought sausages and hot dogs didn't bite.

That's when I saw it. There was a message on it that said, "Use it correctly."

There I was talking to a time machine that could talk! It was extravagant and from the first moment I saw it, it spoke to me.

"Hello Christian! I am a time machine. Let's take a trip to the future."

So I ran and asked my mom if I could go to the future and she said "Sure, honey, just remember to take clean underwear, brush your teeth, and don't forget to do your homework for Teacher Katie."

I got back to my time machine and it was making sounds like this, "nuyn – twooo- achu- peito- hasta la vista." That's when I jumped in and it took me to 3066.

When I got there I said to the first person I met, "Hi. My name is Peito and I am from 2016. I like Nutella."

Then to a few others that gathered, I explained that my time travel was probably a success for the world's intelligence but that I wasn't going to stay and play soccer or four square. Instead I was going to help deal with the world's pollution in 3066.

"Uff!" they all responded. I think that was a good thing.

Everybody is using holographic phones that punctuates their speech with "Muah-Muah." They have artificial organs and kids go to school on hover boards. They are all wearing weird futuristic clothes that actually says, "Hello!" They play a game that is a combination of soccer and football; it's called foccerball! They live in flying houses that are holograms. You know what a hologram is, right? It's like a 3-D picture.

They have no kitchens in the future; they don't eat food. They eat leaves. The future is very different than where I'm from.

Now I'm seeing all the bad stuff that is happening in the world. Everybody is dying. There is one catastrophe after another. Aliens are starting conquests of the Earth. Right now we are the only planet in the solar system.

The ozone cover has been reduced over the years, which means that more of the ultra violet rays are reaching us and it's affecting us badly. Woods are burning and water is evaporating. Every two hours a volcano erupts and every 23 hours an atomic bomb explodes. We are at war with aliens! Meanwhile our planet is moving closer to the sun.

But, I have an idea; it's an idea that can change everything! I'm going to go back in time to fix all of this.

I need to go back in time to fix it all. The burning, the deforestation, the garbage, all the problems.

So I took my time machine and I went back to 2016. I told people what was going to happened in 3066, but they didn't believe it. So, I showed them photos. I started teaching them how to clean up our present day environment, including air pollution, trash, and water pollution.

I even created an organization called Zicacef to fight pollution. But there were some things I couldn't fix such as the depleted ozone layer. But I can help others to learn to stop further depletion of the ozone by reducing, reusing, and recycling. In this way the ozone layer will be saved and the Earth will stop moving towards the sun.

Now I'm going to the future again to see how it's going on there. Hey, I think it'll be alright.

# *Obama in the Future*

Oh no! I could hear the guns outside. The steps sounded closer and closer. When they entered I jumped out of the broken window. I fell and quickly entered the time machine that took me to the future.

My name is Barack Obama, I am from 2016, and I am the actual president of the U.S.A. Everything happened after I gave a speech at the White House about people working on the first time machine and how it was about to be ready. They were already testing it.

It was April 17, 2016. There was a gunman named Marvin and he was so excited that he could kill someone as important as a president. At that point, I was in the control room with five scientists, they controlled the time machine, which I could see from a fragile window. Marvin, along with the terrorists were after us. They wanted the time machine; they also wanted us dead. Then we heard gunfire. I knew the terrorist were here but it was too late. They entered and destroyed everything. They also killed the scientists. They were about to kill me when I jumped out the broken window, entered the time machine, and it took me to 3010.

When I arrived I saw everything flying, as well as lots of Apple stores, and I learned who the new president was. I saw people riding flying cars and other people where on flying sofas so they didn't walk but everything was so peaceful. I wondered who the president of U.S.A. was because when I arrived in New York everything had changed. Times Square was floating. Fifth Avenue was only full of Apple stores and the new president's name was Christopher Vandervelde. The only normal thing was the Statue of Liberty.

In 3010 there was a huge problem! I thought that everything was better in the future but people were destroying nature. All the factories burned coal and this was making horrible air pollution. The people were dying at 35 years old and a bunch of people were dying of cancer of the lungs. Any solutions resulted in worse air. The worst part was that people were selling air for $500 per bottle and people paid it. Also children were dying at 9 years of age because of cancer.

I needed to solve this because it was my fault and I started it. I knew that I needed to stop pollution in the past and save the future. We could save the world but where was I going to find a time machine in New York in 3010? Then I saw one on sale in a store I walked by. I could buy it and turn it on but when I arrived in 2016 all of America would already be destroyed thanks to the terrorist. Everyone was either dead or a slave. I couldn't believe that the present was worse than the future and that there was no solution.

# A Little Less
*Spanish With English Translations*

*Special Thank You*
to *Teachers Maria Cristina Morales and Tamara Arboleda
and our* 4th Grade Typists/Transcribers:
Verónica , Camila, Juan José , and Nicolás

*Special Appreciation*
Spanish stories translated/edited into English
by

Teacher Ericka Arredondo
and
Teacher Isabel Victoria Juliao

1er grado

*La Niña Divertida*

Por: Anelisse Nieto

Había una vez una niña que estaba jugando cerca de un pozo dando vueltas y se estaba mareando.

Después se cayó en el pozo yno podía salir. Buscaron a alguienpero no encontraron a nadie. Después salió del pozo y el papá la ayudó. Salió a salvo pero se raspó, le salió sangre y la limpiaron.

# 1st Grade

## *The Fun Girl*

By: Anelisse Nieto

Once upon a time, there was a girl who was playing near a water well. She was spinning around and she was getting dizzy. Then, she fell into the well but could not get out of it.

People looked for help but they could not find anyone. Later, she came out of the well and her father helped her. She was safe, although, she got some scratches and bled; so they cleaned her up.

## 2do grado

### *El Sistema Solar y Yo*

## Por: David Gonzáles y Matthias Hohner

Había una vez un niño llamado Mateo. Él tenía un sueño. Ese sueño era conocer el sistema solar.

Un día caminaba en el parque y encontró un platillo volador. "WOW" dijo Mateo. Con el platillo volador podré cumplir mi sueño." Él se metió en el platillo y empezó a volar en el sistema solar. Antes de meterse al platillo, compró suficiente gasolina y un casco de oxígeno y lo pagó con el dinero de su papá.

Cuando estaba en Júpiter tenía mucho frío, se acostó y apretó un botón que decía peligro y tomó dirección al sol. Él no sabía qué hacer.

Cada vez Mateo tenía más calor. Mateo apretó un botón que decía súper velocidad.Mateo empezó a gritar tan fuerte que casi rompe un vidrio.

De la nada encontró un cohete que iba a la tierra. Mateo movía la mano diciendo "¡AYUDA!"

Y el astronauta lo vio.

Le dijo a Mateo "Ven, te vamos a ayudar."Mateo saltó de nave en nave y el platillo volador explotó en el sol.Después aterrizó la nave en la tierra y sus padres estaban felices.

Colorín colorete este cuento es un cohete.

Moraleja: Nunca tomes cosas sin permiso.

## 2nd Grade

## The Solar System and Me

## By:David Gonzáles and Matthias Hohner

There was a boy named Mateo. He had a dream. His dream was to get to know the Solar System.

One day, while he was walking in the park he found a space-ship. "Wow" Mateo said, "with this spaceship, I will be able to achieve my dream." He got into the spaceship, and started fly-ing into the Solar System. Before getting in the ship, he bought enough gasoline and an oxygen helmet, and paid for it all with his father's money.

When he was in Jupiter, he was very cold, so he laid down and pushed a button that read DANGER. The spaceship flew towards the sun. The boy didn't know what to do. Mateo was feeling hotter and hotter. Mateo pushed a button that said "su-per speed." He started yelling so loud that he almost broke the glass window.

Out of the blue, a rocket appeared, that was on its way to Earth.Mateo waved his hand yelling "HELP", and the astro-naut saw him. The astronaut told Mateo, "Come, we are going to help you." Mateo jumped from one ship to the other. Then, Mateo's spaceship exploded in the sun.Later on, the rocket landed on the Earth and his parents were very happy.

Moral of the story: Never take something that is not yours.

# 3er grado

### Siguendo los 7 Hábitos

## Por: Hanna Dagga y Laura Jiménez

Había una vez, una niña llamada Eva. Ella no seguía los 7 hábitos en ningún lado. Eva tenia una perra llamada Amy. Eva trataba mal a Amy. Cuando Eva llegó al colegio, Eva no siguió los 7 hábitos. Nunca le hacía caso a su maestra, ni hacía sus cosas. Cuando Eva regresó a su casa pateó a Amy.

Amy se fue y empezó a chillar. Mientras Amy chillaba, Eva le gritó. Eva empezó a ver tele, pero tenía mucha tarea. Al día siguiente, cuando llego al colegio todos los niños estaban felices porque hicieron su tarea, excepto Eva.

Cuando llegó la maestra, llamó a todos los niños para hacerles preguntas. Cuando llamó a Eva, ella se quedó pensando. "¿No practicaste?" preguntó la maestra. "No maestra". La maestra habló con el director. "Ésto no está bien" dijo el director. "Lo siento director, sé que no seguí los 7 hábitos." dijo Eva. "Eso es justo lo que estás haciendo, no estás siguiendo los 7 hábitos."

Entonces, cuando Eva llegó a su casa empezó a jugar con la tabla. No practicó nada y lo mismo pasó el siguiente día, la tuvieron que llevar al director. "Sé más proactiva, no puedes seguir con ésto" dijo el director. Cuando llego al salón, empezó a pensar y no prestó atención.

Cuando regresó a la casa, sacó su cuaderno para hacer la tarea pero no sabía cómo hacer la tarea y empezó a investigar. Cuando llegó al colegio, le dijo a la maestra que sabía todo lo del papel.

"Voy a darte el examen" dijo la maestra. Eva se sintió

preocupada, "Yo, yo no sé nada" dijoEva.La maestra sonrió "Gracias por decir la verdad" dijo la maestra. Y ahora Eva presta mucha atención, es honesta, y todos los niños de la escuela son sus amigos.

Luego cuando llegó a la casa le pidió perdón a Amy. Y Eva la abrazó, Eva empezó a vivir feliz la vida con los 7 hábitos en práctica toda su vida.

Moraleja: Seguir los 7 hábitos en todas partes y con todo el mundo, y nunca trates mal a nadie. Sigue los 7 hábitoste llevarán por el buen camino siempre.

## 3rd Grade

### *Following the 7 Habits*

By: Hanna Dagga and Laura Jiménez

Once upon a time there was a girl named Eva. She did not follow the 7 habits at all. Eva had a dog named Amy. Eva treated Amy badly. When Eva arrived at school, She did not follow the 7 habits. She never obeyed the teacher, nor did her assignments. One day when she returned home, she kicked Amy.

Amy ran away crying. While Amy was crying, Eva yelled at her. Eva started watching TV, but she had a lot of homework to do. On the next day, when Eva arrived at school, all the children were happy because they did their homework; except for her.

When the teacher arrived, she called on all the children to ask them questions. When the teacher called on Eva, she remained pensive. "Didn't you practice?" asked her teacher. "No teacher," she replied. The teacher talked to the principal. "This is not right," said the principal.

"I'm sorry, I know that I did not follow the 7 habits," Eva replied. "That's exactly what you are doing, you are not following the 7 habits!" he returned.

So, when Eva got home, she started playing with her tablet. She didn't practice anything, and the very same thing happened the next day; so they had to take her to the principal's office once again. "Be more proactive," the principal said, "you can't continue like this."

When she arrived to the classroom, she started thinking, but she didn't pay attention. When she got back home, she took her notebook out, but she didn't know how to do it, so she started to research.

When she went to school, she told the teacher that she knew everything that was on the paper. "I am going to give you the test" the teacher said.Eva was worried, "I…I do not know anything," she said. The teacher smiled. "Thanks for telling the truth," she replied.

Now, Eva pays attention, she is honest, and all the children at school are her friends. When she got home, she apologized to Amy, and hugged her. Eva started living her life happily, practicing the 7 habits throughout her lifetime.

Moral of the Story:Follow the 7 habits everywhere and with everyone, and never treat anyone unjustly.Follow the 7 habits, they will take you down a good path at all times!

# 4to grado

## El Pasadizo Secreto

### Por: Camila Quesada y Verónica Yepes

Había una vez una niña que estaba caminando por el pasillo porque estaba sacando copias subiendo las escaleras. De regreso se encontró un botón misterioso en la mitad del pasillo y la curiosidad le ganó y fue a ver que era.

En lo que llego al botón, la campana sonó y se tenía que devolver, pero no lo hizo y tocó el botón rápidamente. El botón desapareció y una puerta apareció. Abrió la puerta y era una luz blanca, y fue a ver que era. "Samanta, Samanta!" gritaba alguien adentro.

Siguió caminando y algo la haló. Llego a un punto donde se perdió. Caminó y caminó y se perdió más. Luego se encontró con un payaso y el payaso le dijo "Sé cómo sacarte de aquí."

Ella se fue con el payaso y era mentira. La empujó a un cuarto y la encerró. Poco después sedio cuenta que no estaba sola y habían otras niñas de la escuela.

Tiempo después las niñas descubrieron como salir del cuarto. Se tardaron tiempo en salir de allí pero al final lograron hacerlo.

Las 3 niñas salieron corriendo al salón y en lo que llegaron sonó el despertador. Samanta se despertó y estaba asustada. Luego se dio cuenta que todo era solo un sueño y que no se había quedado encerrada en un pasillo.

Moraleja: No confíes en los extraños.

# 4th Grade

## *The Secret Passage*

### By:Camila Quesada and Verónica Yepes

There was once a girl who was walking through the school hall because she was getting some copies upstairs. On the way back, she found a mysterious button in the middle of the hall; curiosity won her over and she went to find out what it was. As soon as she got near the button, the bell rang and she had to return to class, but instead she touched the button swiftly. The button disappeared and a door appeared. She opened the door and out came a white light, which she went to see what it was.

"Samantha, Samantha!" shouted someone inside. She kept walking and something pulled her in. It came to a point where she was lost. She walked and walked and got even more lost. Afterward, she met a clown and the clown told her "I know how to get you out of here."

So, she followed the clown, but he was lying. He pushed her into a room and locked her in. A bit after, she realized she was not alone and there were other girls from her school as well.

Sometime after, the girls figured out how to get out of the room. It took them a long time to get out of there, but in the end, they were able to. The 3 girls left running towards the classroom and as soon as they arrived, the alarm clock sounded.

Samantha woke up and was scared. She then realized that it was all a dream and that she had not been locked up inside a hall.

Moral of the Story: Do not trust strangers.

## 5to grado

### *La Termita Come Metal*

## Por: Christian Vandervelde y José Yepes

Hace muy poco tiempo había una pequeña termita pero ella era especial, ella podía comer metal.

Siempre se entretenía comiendo metal de un auto viejo, pero ella era la única que tenía esa capacidad. El resto de las termitas se burlaban de ella por no comer madera. Un día la termita encontró un carro de un exterminador, inteligentemente regresó al hormiguero para advertir a las demás pero ninguna le creyó.

Pero al día siguiente volvióa revisar el carro del exterminador, y se encontró con dos exterminadores. Los escuchó hablar sobre exterminar a todas las termitas que encontraran. Nuevamente se volvió al hormiguero pero esta vez le advirtió a la reina termita y ella si la escuchó e inmediatamente advirtió a los guerreros. Los guerreros fueron guiados por la termita. Pero inmediatamente llamaron la atención de los hombres, los hombres rápidamente agarraron sus armas, muchas termitas intentaron atacar pero murieron en el intento, todas sus armas eran de metal y la única termita que quedaba era la come metal. Rápidamente empezó a morder las armas de los hombres que quedaron desarmados.

Nunca había visto una termita con la habilidad de comer metal, la termita mordió y mordió todo lo que le parecía rico. Al día siguiente, todos los de el hormiguero le tenían respeto, entonces se sintió muy sola.

La termita sabía que la única manera que encajara era

aprendiendo a comer madera, pero sus dientes hacían que le costara más. Días tras días, invierno tras invierno, primavera tras primavera, otoño tras otoño la termita aprendió a comer madera pero días después cuando la termita comía madera se murió en instantes después.

Un fin grande para un sueño pequeño.

Moraleja: Siempre esforzarse para alcanzar tus metas y respetar las diferencias de los demás.

# 5th Grade

## *The Metal Eating Termite*

By: Christan Vandervelde and José Yepes

Not very long ago, there was a little termite but she was special; she was able to eat metal. She was always entertained by eating the metal of an old automobile, but she was the only one in her anthill with those skills. The rest of the termites made fun of her because she did not eat wood. One day, the termite found an exterminator's car. Smartly, she went back to the anthill to warn the other termites, but the others didn't believe her.

The next day, she went to check on the exterminator's car, and she ran into two exterminators. She heard them talking about exterminating all of the termites that they could find. Once again, she went back to the anthill but this time she warned the Queen termite. The Queen in turn, did listen to her and immediately warned the warriors. The warriors were guided by the termite. But they immediately caught the attention of the exterminators, who quickly grabbed their weapons. Many termites tried to attack but died in their intent.All of their weapons were made of metal and the only termite left was the one that could eat metal. Rapidly, she started to chew the men's weapons which eventually got disarmed. They had never seen a termite with such a metal eating skill. She chewed and chewed everything that appeared tasty. The next day, everyone in the anthill respected her, she then felt very lonely.

The termite knew that the only way to fit in was by learning to eat wood, but her teeth made it difficult for her.Day after day, winter after winter, spring after spring, fall after fall, the termite finally learned how to eat wood. But days after the termite learned to eat wood, she died shortly after.

A big end to a small dream.

Moral of the Story:Always work to reach your goals, and respect differences of others.

# Meet the Teachers

*Teacher Tamara Arboleda,* who was inspired to teach by a nun, started teaching in 1998. Before teaching social studies and Spanish at Boston School, she taught the same subjects at Oxford International. She says she watched through a window this one Catholic nun "teach a classroom full of kids." That's when Ms. Arboleda knew teaching was for her. She earned a BA in Humanities with a specialization in Spanish at the University of Panama. In her spare time she enjoys doing handcrafts like Tembleques. (It's the headdress used for a national folkloric dress called the Pollera.) Ms. Arboleda also enjoys organizing parties. When she was in primary school she recalls being "very talkative, but well behaved." As a student, she always enjoyed writing, the arts, and Spanish. And as a teacher, she wants to always make sure that "my students acquire knowledge in a fun and enjoyable way."

*Teacher Erika Arredondo* has been teaching English for twelve years. First in her homeland of Colombia at Gimnasio los Cerezos, Centro Colombo Americano, and Universidad Autonoma de Manizales. In 2010 she started working here in Panama at Oxford International School, teaching 2nd and 5th grade math, then 2nd grade homeroom for two years. She joined BSI this year and has been working as an in-house substitute teacher.

*Teacher Michelle Barrios* started her teaching career in 2004. Before that she tutored kids to make some money while she was attending college studying computer engineering. "I ended up liking teaching so much," that she changed her major to English Literature, and she's never looked back or questioned that decision. Since joining one of the world's oldest, most respected professions, she's taught first, second, and third grades. In her free time, when she's not teaching or currently working towards her master's degree in bilingual education, she loves watching documentaries. As a third grader herself, she admits her reading wasn't fluent. Her writing wasn't much better. She couldn't tell time or memorize her times tables. "I struggled," she recalls now. She still remembers her third grade teacher as very judgmental, who didn't take the time to help students when they needed it. Ms. Barrios has overcome many of her primary deficits in learning. For one thing, today she's an impeccable speller in both Spanish and English. When she was a child in primary school she didn't like how most teachers played favorites; that's why as a teacher today she makes sure she is fair and caring to all her students, working extra hard to make sure each one them receive the very best in teaching from her.

*Teacher Mindy Cooper* currently teaches first grade at Boston School International in Panama. She started in education in 2009 as a P.E. Teacher. Since then, she's flex her muscle, teaching K-8th as a homeroom teacher, 6-12th as a Spanish teacher and 5th through 9th as a special needs teacher. Before she got into teaching, she traveled the world for a popular TV show, but eventually grew weary of that kind of nomadic lifestyle that she called "The Circus". No clowning around, she thinks she might have been a "pain in the neck" with all the questions she asked her 1st grade teacher, Ms Fox (Not sure International Baccalaureate was around then!). She loved everything about elementary school and had inklings of her future career as an educator when she'd spend countless childhood hours teaching her teddy bears. She's currently working on her Masters degree in primary education with a minor in developmental reading and writing. Previously she earned Bachelor degrees in social and human studies and education. With all her free time in the future, she plans on pursuing her PhD in primary administration, which she hopes to complete in three years. Good luck (future doctor) Mindy!

*Teacher Myriam DePuy* is in her second year teaching at Boston School International. She's been teaching since 1983. She's taught in a variety of grade levels, but likes primary the best. Ms. DePuy holds a BA degree in political science from Ohio Dominican College (USA) and a master's degree in English language from Universidad de la Paz. Prior to joining BSI, she taught high school at The Oxford School, also in Panama, and before that, Cuernovaca in Mexico. As a child she attended the Chiquita Brand School in Puerto Armuelles, Chirique. As a second grader and beyond she says, "I loved learning." Her superb spoken English comes from all the American teachers who taught her throughout primary. One of her favorite subjects was and is writing. Forever young, Ms. DePuy, who volunteers after school at her husband's small veterinarian clinic, plans on staying in the teaching business for some time to come. "I love teaching. At my age, I'm still enjoying working with kids."

*Teacher Joseph A. Haviland* is in his first year of teaching at Boston School International, which he calls "a delightful private school in Panama that's got heart and soul." But he's been teaching since 1998. This is his fourth year of teaching 4th grade in Panama City, Panama. He and his wife, Alicia, are high-caliber international teachers who have taught in the United Sates, Costa Rica, Venezuela, Mexico, as well as Panama. Mr. Haviland holds a BA degree in Journalism and History from New York University. After a brief stint as a public access TV talk show host of the eponymous-named *The Joe Haviland Show, Where Everybody's a Star,*in Los Angeles, CA, he earned an MS degree in Elementary Education from the University of Bridgeport in Connecticut. And he's particularly proud of his Certificate from the University of Washington (in Seattle) in Advanced Literary Fiction. He's one of eleven children (lucky #7) born to Chauncey and Muriel Haviland. His teacher for fourth grade was Ms. Marcelino and it was at Chatsworth Elementary School in Larchmont, NY, where he spent most of his childhood. His most precious moment in education? When he was working as a substitute teacher, on a cold snowy morning in the desert of Albuquerque, NM, he mentioned the hamburger chain, Red Robin, and his young charismatic charges broke into a spontaneously loud and sustained, "Yum!"


*Teacher Isabel Victoria Juliao* started her education career path in 2003 as an on-call substitute for Balboa Academy. In 2005, she became a PK4 homeroom teacher for The Oxford School. She says she was "blessed with my first daughter at a young age." As a result she put her studies on hold, eventually returning to school. In 2008 she received her Bachelor's degree in International Affairs, then worked for the US Embassy and

Ministry of Foreign Affairs Panama, but nothing proved as fulfilling or enriching as her work as a teacher. "Motherly love is what brought me into this field," with her daughter being her first student. She's currently the mother of two wonderful girls, ages 15 and 4. Since 2009 she's worked as a homeroom teacher for grades Pre-K, Kindergarten, 1st , 2nd , and 3rd. Ms. Juliao is currently a substitute and support teacher for Boston School International. "I enjoy music and dancing very much. In my teenage years I played the saxophone, which then lead me to play for the UCF marching band, and eventually a local band in my early 20s." She also loves to surf. A well-behaved student in elementary school, "I loved my 4th grade teacher Maria Dillon. I was one of those strange kids who really enjoyed school." Writing was definitely something that she loved to do, so she's excited about this book of student writing. Her future in education?"I want to inspire children to enjoy learning by using varied techniques to respect their unique learning methods."


*Teacher Katie Lamb* is from the United States of America, and has enjoyed living in Panama for the last 3 years, with her husband who is from Panama originally and moved back to study medicine. Originally from Kansas City, Missouri, where she grew up as the 4th of 6 kids. She has a passion for sports, especially American football and baseball. She moved to Utah after high school to attend the University of Utah, where she was initially studying cellular biology, until she took a job at a local elementary school, and realized she wanted to work with kids. From there she switched her degree to elementary education, and knowing she would be working with English language learners here in Panama acquired her TEFL certification. She loves teaching, and watching kids get excited about what they are learning, and seeing them realize that learning is fun and exciting.

*Teacher Joselibeth Medina* believes that "education for me is one of the most important pillars in my life." She studied early stimulation and family counseling "because it is one of the careers that works to develop the skills of children from an early age." Ms. Medina started working in a child development center, and was responsible for a group of children, ages 1 to 3 years old. Ms. Medina called it "a very enriching experience. Then, she decided to go to the USA to study English. When she returned she had an opportunity to work as a PK3 homeroom teacher. "I have had other experiences as an English teacher which have helped me grow." She currently works as a substitute teacher for Boston School International.

*Teacher Ruth Mendoza* currently teaches computer here at BSI, traveling a more than a mile each day from classroom to classroom with her special computer cart on wheels, full of wonderful laptop technology for all students (K-12) to utilize at various times during the school week. She's also directing the nascent PYP program in International Baccalaureate for primary grades here at Boston School International.

*Teacher Maria Cristina Morales* started teaching in 1999. She currently teaches Spanish to primary students at Boston School, as well as social studies. She has taught at four different schools in Panama, also as a computer and homeroom teacher, teaching all subjects. She's particularly proud of her family (husband and two children). When not teaching she enjoys dancing to all kinds of musical genres. She remembers her kindergarten teacher, Yessenia, who she says was "sweet and loved to sing. She was a very simple and caring person." When she was in elementary school as a student, Ms. Morales liked having just one teacher for all her subjects.

*Teacher Elsie Soto* currently teaches first grade with energy and enthusiasm at Boston School International in Panama. For her, teaching is a "rewarding experience full of challenges, learning and affection."

*Teacher (Juan) Manuel Vinueza* is a native of Panama who started teaching in 1980 after completing his university degree. The best part of teaching for him is that he gets to make a difference in sharing good moral values with his pupils. Before joining the impeccable Boston School staff, he taught at Oxford International School. Prior to that he taught at Instituto Episcopal. As a second grader himself he remembers being very quiet and respectful. He loved drawing and writing about his drawings as a primary student. A dedicated disco dancer (Stayin' Alive), he once was a Taekwondo instructor. He wants to keep teaching in the years ahead, "showing good manners in the classroom."

# Epilogue for Dr. Frederic K. Gornell

Gone but *Not* Forgotten, Ever!

"I'll remember a leader who always had time to talk, guide, and express his feelings about what he expected from teachers and students. He was ready to listen to our comments, problems and suggestions about any concern we might have at any moment. I'm so grateful to God for giving me a chance to work with him. Yes, a leader and a friend, Frederic Gornell."
- *Carlos Palau, BSI Middle School Math Teacher*

"He loved animals but not in captivity. Running free in the wild. He stopped eating meat because of the suffering they go through before and when they are killed, including the chicks that are made into chicken nuggets."
- *Isabel Sierra, BSI Kindergarten Teacher*

"Yo conocí al Sr. Gornell en el 2005. Él era una persona muy buena y buen jefe. Él era más que todo un amigo porque siempre estaba dispuesto a ayudarnos."
- *Yamileth Sánchez, BSI Custodian*

"Frederic Gornell, muy buena persona, muy amable, muy amigo de todos. Lo conocí cuando entré a la escuela. Lo siento como amigo no como jefe."
- *Gloria Beitia, BSI Custodian*

"Yo lo conocí en el 2013. Él era una buena persona y tenía mucha confianza en el personal. Cubría los valores de respeto y confianza."

*- Laura Guevara, BSI Librarian*


"An impeccable man who I was looking forward to knowing more over time and space. It was my first year at BSI, so I had known Frederic for less than a year. But believe me when I say he saved me from an uncertain fate; he lifted me out of a particularly languishing teaching moment in my career as an educator. I remember sitting with him in his office a short time before his death, and him positively informing me about his upcoming back and shoulder surgery stateside. It proved a surgery he wouldn't return from. The moment staff at BSI found out about his demise was dark and somber; for weeks/months the shock of it lingered. If I had known that this would be my last meeting with Frederic, I'd have spent a few more moments chatting with him, telling him how much I appreciated him, relishing our last conversation. I took it for granted that he would be back! Now I try to take nothing for granted. All we have is this moment. ¡Hasta luego, mano! See you in that place we all go to after life."

*- Joseph Haviland, BSI Primary Teacher*


"Que difícil me resulta sintetizar en pocas líneas recuerdos del Sr. Gornell o Doc. como acostumbraba al dirigirme a él. Su valor humano, su sensibilidad estarán presentes en mis recuerdos; fui testigo al ver estudiantes, acudientes y colaboradores llegar a su oficina con una inconformidad y salir de ella sonrientes y satisfechos por el respeto y la forma en que manejaba cada inconveniente. Mi agradecimiento eterno por todas las enseñanzas que dejo en mí, por su amistad y cariño."

*- Marly Ferraz Fleites, BSI PE Teacher*


"I didn't know Mr. Gornell for as long as others might have, but I will be forever grateful at the opportunity he gave me to work for him. Not only did it feel like I was getting a job, but it felt like he was trusting me and my abilities, regardless of my age and years of experience. I felt incredibly valued and rewarded whenever I spoke with him."

*- Kheriah VanEijs, BSI Middle School English Teacher*


"Yo llegué a conocerlo por 16 años. De los 16 años que lo conocí, para mí era una persona con mucha sabiduría. Seguí su ejemplo pues era una persona inspiradora y era más que un jefe y amigo."

*- Daniel Rivera, BSI Custodian*


"I thank God for having had the opportunity to work side by side with my beloved cousin Butchie, as we called him in the family. We always had a very special relationship, but working with him and being with him every day, made me know him even better and see what a wonderful and kind man he was. I could witness for myself how everyone in the school, students, teachers, and staff loved him dearly and that gives me a great satisfaction and pride to have had him in my family and to have felt him so near. May God have you in His glory, my dear Butchie."

*- Sally Calvo, BSI Secretary*

"Fue una persona excepcional, un hombre con gran sentimiento humanitario. Lo sentía como un lider. Lo conocí en septiembre de 2013 cuando empecé a trabajar en la escuela. Es un ejemplo a seguir."

*- Marta De la Cruz, BSI Cafeteria Worker*


"Lo conocí en el colegio. Era muy buena persona. Era muy cordial también. Lo siento como un amigo. Hablabamos bastante. Era una persona con muchos valores."

*- Roberto Squires, BSI Custodian*


"Lo conocí en Noviembre del 2014. Era una buena persona, jefe y amigo. Lo siento como un compañero. Lo conocí en la entrevista. Principalmente cubría respeto y amabilidad ante todoslos valores."

*- Maribel Aguilar, BSI Secretary*


"Frederick Gornell was my mentor and dear friend. He was a great man who not only contributed to the improvement of Panamanian education but also touched the lives of many including my own. I will be forever grateful as he gave me the the opportunity to become an educator, setting me out on a lifetime journey. I will miss him tremendously but he will always live in the hearts of all who had the privilege to know him."

*- Ana Woodward, BSI High School Coordinator*

"I believe in destiny, therefore I really think I was meant to meet Mr. Gornell and work with him. He encouraged me to take a position in teaching middle school at Boston School International. His words still sound in my head, 'You are going to love it.' I certainly do, but what I love most is that I had the opportunity to work by his side. He was a great, kind, and sweet man who was always available for all of us; he will be missed forever!"

*- Keyla Lopez, BSI MS Teacher*

"En la vida el compromiso es tan importante. Así lo logré ver en esta agradable persona durante catorce años, preocupado por la educación de muchas generaciones que a lo largo del tiempo he visto pasar. Hoy muchos profesionales están agradecidos por alcanzar sus metas. El Señor Gornell en momentos difíciles en que muchas veces se encontró, supo salir con la frente en alto buscando solución en diferentes circunstancias. Como Director su esfuerzo refleja hoy su historia."

*- Santana González, BSI Custodian*

Editor's Note: If you don't speak/read/write Spanish, check out this website: http://www.spanishdict.com/translation, which bills itself, "Instant English-Spanish translation from the most trusted Spanish translator." You can cut and paste anything in Spanish in this picture-pretty website and it translates it to English (and vice versa/al revés), more or less.

Book Cover Art Created

by

Fourth Grade (2016)

Students

@

BSI

In the Art Class

of

Teacher Bonnie DeFamiglietti

whose indefatigable, creative direction is evident every day

in her role as both Art and Music teacher at BSI.

Whenever I stop by her "classroom" and see this

tireless teacher and her joyful students at work,

along with their projects,

I think of Santa's workshop!

**All good things come to an end.**

人无千日好

花无百日红

rén wú qiān rì hǎo
huā wú bǎi rì hóng

Lightning Source UK Ltd.
Milton Keynes UK
UKOW01f2206261016

286242UK00001B/33/P

9 781478 777489